The Spy with the Wooden Leg
THE STORY OF VIRGINIA HALL

Nancy Polette

Alma Little
St Paul, Minnesota

Cover painting "Les Marguerites Fleuriront ce Soir" courtesy of Jeffrey W. Bass, artist. CIA Fine Art Collection. Cloistered in an old barn in south central France, OSS spy Virginia Hall communicates with London. Edmond Lebret (cousin of Leah Lebret), a Maquis leader, operates an improvised, manual generator to supply power to Virginia's B2 spy radio. The code phrase *les marguerites fleuriront ce soir* (the daisies will bloom tonight) alerts Virginia to expect something from London.

Library of Congress Cataloging-in-Publication Data
Polette, Nancy.
   The spy with the wooden leg : the story of Virginia Hall / by Nancy Polette.
      p.cm.
   Includes bibliographical references.
   ISBN 978-1-934617-15-1 (hardcover)--ISBN 978-1-934617-16-8 (pbk.)
   1. Goillot, Virginia, 1906-1982 --Juvenile literature. 2. Women spies--United States--Biography--Juvenile literature. 3. Spies--United States--Biography--Juvenile literature. 4. Intelligence officers--United States--Biography--Juvenile literature. 5. World War, 1939-1945--Secret service--United States--Juvenile literature. 6. World War, 1939-1945--Underground movements--France--Juvenile literature. I. Title.
   UB271.U52G64 2012
   940.54'8673092--dc23
                     2012007281
              Printed in United States of America
                       1 2 3 4 5
         Alma Little is an imprint of Elva Resa Publishing LLC
         8362 Tamarack Vlg Ste 119-106 St Paul, MN 55125
                     http://www.almalittle.com
         A portion of book sales is donated to charity.

CONTENTS

PREFACE

Something very special happened in the year 1906 in the United States. It was the same year the Fuller Brush Company had its beginnings. The same year Sears, Roebuck and Co. opened the largest business building in the world for its mail order catalog plant. The first radio broadcast of voice and music aired from Brant Rock, Massachusetts. President Theodore Roosevelt proclaimed Devils Tower the nation's first national monument. It was during this exciting time in history, on April 6, 1906, Virginia Hall was born.

Twelve days after Virginia's birth, a major earthquake struck San Francisco and the coast of Northern California. The fires that burned out of control afterward destroyed ninety percent of the city. Who could have predicted that, thirty-four years later, Virginia Hall would prove to be more damaging and destructive to the German Gestapo than any earthquake? Virginia, nicknamed Dindy by her older brother, John, would become known by many names in her life. The French Resistance leaders of World War II called her *la dame qui boite* or the Limping Lady. To the German Gestapo, she was known as Artemis, and labeled one of the most dangerous Allied spies in France.

How did a young woman from a wealthy Baltimore family, born at a time when daughters led sheltered lives and a woman's place was in the home, become one of the bravest and most valued intelligence agents in World War II? This is Virginia Hall's story.

NOTE FROM THE AUTHOR

The following is a true account of the life of Virginia Hall and her work as an international spy. This biography is slightly fictionalized where I have created dialogue for Virginia, her family, and those with whom she worked. With the exception of written reports, we can never know the exact words spoken by Virginia, leaders of the Special Operations Executive (SOE), other American and British agents, and leaders of the French Resistance; however, I have made every effort to be faithful to the character of each speaker based on letters, journals, reports, and anecdotal accounts in order to bring alive the unique character of this extraordinary woman. Virginia Hall was a fearless, responsible, extremely well-organized, capricious, unpredictable, highly intelligent leader who did not suffer fools gladly. The portions of this biography that deal with her espionage work for the SOE and Office of Strategic Services (OSS) are well documented through her actual written reports.

CHAPTER 1

The Dream

"LOOK OUT, CONSULATE, HERE I COME!"

Startled passengers stepped out of the way as the slender, freckle-faced, twenty-seven-year-old woman flew down the aisle, grabbing the arm of the nearest tattered seat as the smoke-blackened train jerked to a stop. Smyrna, Turkey!

Virginia Hall was eager for her next assignment. She knew it would bring her one step closer to making her dream come true, a dream that began when she was fourteen years old.

The wealthy Hall family had been on holiday in London, taking in the sights in Grosvenor Square, when Virginia looked west to see the sprawling American embassy, sunlight sparkling off its dozens and dozens of windows. The three-story building stretched out for nearly a city block. It was the office of the American ambassador to the Court of St. James, the personal representative of the president of the United States. Virginia grinned and gave a quick salute to the embassy. One day, she planned to reside there—or in one like it in another country. She wanted to travel to foreign lands, representing the president. She would meet with foreign dignitaries and help resolve conflicts among nations. She would become the first woman ambassador! When her father pointed out there were no women ambassadors, Virginia assured him it was time there were, and she would lead the way.

After years of learning foreign languages, bombarding the US State Department with letters, filling out dozens of forms, and undergoing FBI investigations, Virginia was assigned her first overseas job at the American embassy in Warsaw, Poland, in 1931. And now, two years later, she was ready to prove how invaluable she could be to the consular service in Smyrna.

An ancient Maxwell pulled into the station. The driver spotted his passenger, the tall, slender Virginia, waiting on the rickety platform. A light wind tossed her shoulder-length brown hair into tangles.

"Miss Hall?" the driver's booming voice echoed as he brought the Maxwell to a stop. Virginia watched a big, lumbering fellow climb out of the car. His hair was faded blond with streaks of gray, bits of it sticking out from under his hat.

"Welcome to Smyrna," the man said, grinning and vigorously shaking her hand up and down like a pump handle. "I'm Crosby, Consul George's aide."

Before Virginia could say hello, the friendly giant lifted her trunk and tossed it in the boot of the embassy car. "After you," he said, whipping open the door to reveal tattered seats with ragged edges and rips that had been clumsily sewn together.

A turn of the key brought a sharp backfire. Black smoke poured from the tailpipe. Crosby shook his head in exasperation as he nursed the tired engine to life. "New cars in Turkey are as scarce as hen's teeth, so we make do with Old Faithful here." He gave the dashboard an affectionate pat.

Crosby steered the old car through the heart of the city, past the clock tower in Konak Square. The elaborate clock was a long-ago gift from the Germans. Leaving the tower in the distance, neither Virginia nor Crosby could guess that Germany's gift-giving days were over.

"Your new home," Crosby told her, pulling up to a two-story, white-plastered building. Lifting her black leather trunk from the boot as if weightless, he led her to a two-room flat on the first floor.

"Not exactly fancy," Crosby said, "but only two blocks from the consulate. You'll want to settle in today. Tomorrow is soon enough to start work. Oh, and don't be late. The boss likes his staff to be on time."

The main room was small with a horsehair couch and a round table covered with rose-patterned oilcloth.

There was a dry sink along one wall and next to it a small stove. The second room contained a single iron bed and wooden chest. The heavy curtains held the faint odor of cigarette smoke. The only decoration Virginia added as she unpacked was a small photograph of her family's Box Horn Farm. She tacked it up just above the sink. Then, tired from her journey, she fell asleep for the night.

The following morning, Virginia checked her appearance in the cracked vanity mirror. Smooth skin required little makeup. A light dusting of powder over her high cheekbones and determined chin was all she needed.

Dressed in a spotless shirtwaist, tweed skirt, and matching jacket, she slipped on sensible spectator pumps. Heeding Crosby's warning, she arrived at her new job thirty minutes early.

Walking through the consulate doors, Virginia entered another world. Here was faded old-world elegance with antique brass lamps and heavy chairs covered with leather or velvet. Carpets woven by master craftsmen showed the wear of many years of tramping feet. On the walls, replicas of the old masters stared down at visitors. Despite the worn appearance, the reception hall had a certain charm.

Anxious to find out what her duties were, Virginia found Crosby. He led her to a small two-drawer oak desk on which sat a tall stack of memos and letters and a very large, very old Remington typewriter.

"It's all yours," Crosby quipped, pointing to the typewriter. "It is almost as old as Old Faithful," he said, laughing as he lumbered over to his own desk.

Virginia stared at the huge pile of memos and letters waiting to be typed. No one had asked about her typing skills. She had none. She glared at the typewriter. In her eyes the enemy machine took on human form, challenging her to fail.

"No machine gets the best of me," she muttered. She whipped out a sheet of paper, rolled it into the machine, and set to work punching keys one finger at a time.

Twelve hours later, with blistered fingertips and aching hands, she pulled the last letter out of the typewriter. The wastebasket by her desk held dozens of wadded up sheets of paper. The consulate was silent. The cleaning ladies, usually the last to leave, had gone home. Virginia rose and stretched her arms above her head, relieving the tight ache between her shoulders. She picked up her bag, reached for her coat, and paused. The door to the ambassador's office was open. Overwhelmed with curiosity, she could not resist the urge to explore.

A soft, plush, burgundy carpet led to a gleaming, glass-topped desk clear of papers from the day's work, leaving only a framed photo of the ambassador's family. Virginia kicked off her shoes and slid her feet across soft pile, making her way toward the ambassador's oversized brown leather chair. She reached out, gave it a spin, and heard a protesting squeak. Unable to resist the temptation, she sank down into the soft leather folds and let out a satisfied sigh. One day this chair, or one like it in another consulate, would be hers—even if she had to type a thousand memos to get there.

Despite her lack of typing and clerical skills, within a month Virginia became a favorite of Consul W. Perry George. In a written report, he stated she was "absolutely reliable with a good sense of responsibility, very conscientious and helpful, with a charming personality."

In fact, Virginia proved to be so capable, she was often given duties usually reserved for Foreign Service officers.

It was a bitter cold day in late November when Virginia's language skills were put to good use. Overnight, Smyrna was blanketed with a foot of snow. Even though Virginia lived close by, the snow slowed the city and she arrived late at the consulate. She heard loud voices as she opened the door.

"What's the trouble?" she asked the receptionist. An excited man jumped up and down, waving his arms in the air. He pointed to the street. He made a motion like snow coming down. He smacked his hands together, all the time speaking as loudly as he could.

Virginia understood. The man was speaking French. He and his wife were traveling in their small Fiat when it was hit by a much larger touring car. His wife was injured and taken to a hospital. The authorities detained him for questioning. He did not know where they had taken his wife. He did not know how badly she might have been hurt.

"Please," Virginia said, "sit here." She pointed to a comfortable, velvet-upholstered chair near her desk. She spoke quietly to the man in French. She would find his wife.

It took only a few phone calls. His wife was not badly injured. He could come get her. With directions to the hospital in his hand, the man left the consulate, bowing his thanks again and again.

The consulate at Smyrna, known for its hospitality, had frequent visitors. One of these was Secretary of State Cordell Hull. Watching the way Virginia put visitors at ease, he told the ambassador Virginia could "become a fine career girl in the consular service."

With such a high recommendation, Virginia applied to take the Foreign Service examination, the next step in her goal of becoming the first woman ambassador. She filled out form after form and sent them off to the US State Department in Washington, DC. She was sure she would soon be on her way to fulfilling her dream.

CHAPTER 2

The Dream Postponed

What Virginia missed most about home were the lush green forests of the family's Box Horn Farm where she and her brother, John, usually spent their summers. Just outside Smyrna were forests teeming with wildlife, so Virginia did not hesitate to say yes when asked by two coworkers to join a hunting party. They would be hunting snipe in Turkey's woodlands, thirty kilometers from Smyrna.

December 8, 1933, dawned with a bright sun and a crisp breeze. In the group were Virginia, two male coworkers from the consulate, the wife of one, and a Turkish guide. The guide took a heavy basket from Virginia.

"Careful with that," she said, laughing. "It's our lunch." From the local shops that morning, Virginia had purchased cold sliced lamb, pasta, figs, dates, and fresh-baked bread with honey.

The party would picnic in the country and go snipe hunting in the afternoon when the short-legged, long-billed chunky birds were most likely to be seen. It had been a long time since those days at the farm when

Virginia had handled a gun. But she knew those early shooting lessons with her father would stay with her.

The group moved quietly through the shadowy green marsh. The air was chill and damp. One man sneezed. The others gave him scolding looks. The slightest noise could frighten away the black-and-brown-feathered birds. The eagle-eyed hunters scanned the marshes, searching for the game birds that often gathered on mud flats. The only sound, "RIBBET, RIBBET, RIBBET," was the occasional croak of a frog answered by other croaks nearby.

Moving quietly, Virginia left the group to seek out the birds on her own. Soft, wet mud squished beneath her boots, making a sucking sound as she lifted one foot then the other. She wrinkled her nose at the familiar smell of rotting leaves and oozing muck. Her acute hearing caught the slightest rustle of leaves or grass. The guide had told the team to be on the lookout for wolves, red foxes, dangerous wild boars, or even an occasional black bear. Instructions were to shoot the wild boar but to back slowly away from the bear.

She carried her twelve-gauge shotgun, barrel pointing down, as she had been taught to do. Virginia watched for movement in the tall reeds, listening intently for the slightest rustle that might indicate snipes. Suddenly her foot slipped into a muddy hole, twisting her ankle.

"Aaiiee!" she cried out as pain shot through her like hot needles. The shotgun slipped from her grasp and she made a clumsy grab, barely keeping it from slipping into the wet marsh even as she struggled not to fall into the mud herself.

In the next moment, the shotgun went off with a deafening boom, and Virginia screamed from the agonizing pain of shotgun pellets shattering her left foot. She crumpled to the ground.

Drifting in and out of consciousness, Virginia heard the rushing footsteps of horrified friends. Pain throbbed through her entire body. She was so cold. Hands she couldn't see were touching her, and she heard faraway voices.

"Bleeding . . . in shock . . . we've got to keep her warm . . . hospital. . ."

First aid supplies were back in the car. Virginia felt a coat draped across her legs. She heard the tearing of cloth. Knife-like pains shot up her leg from the injured foot as pressure was applied to stop the bleeding.

Voices came from a distance. "Looks bad . . . overcoat for stretcher . . . hurry . . ."

Gentle hands rolled Virginia over and back, laying her on a large overcoat. She felt herself lifted from the cold ground. The makeshift stretcher swayed back and forth as the men struggled uphill through the heavy brush, now and then slipping on the damp leaves. At last, they emerged from the gray and misty marsh. The air was lighter. The heavy odor of wet moss and slimy earth was gone.

"Careful . . . steady . . . easy now . . ." Again, the faint words came from a distance, then faded away as Virginia lost consciousness. The drive to the hospital in Smyrna took more than an hour.

Examining Virginia's mangled foot, the doctors shook their heads. The affected area was swollen. Mud and stagnant marsh water had seeped into the terrible wound, producing a foul odor. Within the blackened pellet holes, infection was beginning to set in. There were no antibiotics in 1933. Signs of gangrene, a serious blood poisoning, were likely to soon appear.

Dr. Lorrin Shepard, the American surgeon, was sent for from Istanbul. After one look at the terrible wound, he knew what had to be done. Waiting to see if the wound would improve was dangerous. It showed every sign of getting worse.

He spoke to a half-conscious Virginia. His words were gentle, but his message was brutal. "You will have to lose part of your leg. There is no choice. It's your leg or your life."

Virginia heard the words as if from a long distance. Through a haze of pain, she saw the kind doctor's face.

She nodded that she understood.

Doctors amputated the injured leg below the knee.

Hours later, Virginia woke to stiff, scratchy sheets, the powerful smell of antiseptic, and overwhelming pain that shot up her leg like a hot poker, through her body like a twisted slice of a knife. Heavily drugged, day after day, her half-world was one of dozing and awakening, of dizziness and nausea and pain. Doctors came and went, examining the site of the amputation again and again. Nurses changed the dressings daily, keeping a watchful eye for any sign of infection.

With the passing of the second week, Dr. Shepard breathed a sigh of relief. The wound was clean. The infection had not taken hold. Good news? Yes! But for Virginia, there was little relief from the constant searing, burning pain. Even for the tough and resilient Dindy, day after day of unending torture proved almost too much. Her dreams were forgotten. Every moment was taken with fighting the overwhelming pain. She barely recognized staff members from the embassy who came and went, shocked at her gaunt appearance. The dark circles under her eyes and her one-syllable responses added to their concern. The spirited Virginia they knew seemed to have departed along with her leg.

CHAPTER 3

Recovery

By mid-January, Virginia's health had improved enough that she was transferred to the American Hospital in Istanbul. The waves of pain in her healing stump had lessened to ripples. Food looked good again. The old Virginia emerged from a pain-wracked cocoon. Despite any discouragement she may have felt by the loss of her leg, she had not abandoned her dream. It had only been postponed for a time.

With the passing of another month, she felt new energy. Slowly but surely, she gained back the weight lost during those earlier hazy, bedridden weeks. The dark circles under her eyes disappeared; the gray pallor of her skin gave way to touches of healthy pink.

Among the possessions Crosby packed up and brought from her flat was the photograph of Box Horn Farm. As Virginia stared at the photo, she lifted her determined chin and came eye to eye with Dr. Shepard. "I beat the State Department, and the typewriter, and I'll beat this leg!" she said. "I'm going home."

Dr. Shepard laughed. He didn't know what she meant

by beating the typewriter, but there was no mistaking her resolve to get well. He agreed she was well enough to travel back to the States.

Within a week, Virginia booked passage on the first ship sailing from London to Boston. The woman on crutches, making the early morning rounds of the deck, became a familiar sight to fellow passengers. Virginia was committed to getting back her strength. Exercise was key!

Arriving at the Boston pier, she refused offers of help and managed with little difficulty the transfer from the ship to the train that carried her to Baltimore. She had told no one, not even her mother, of her arrival. She refused to be coddled or pampered.

The taxi ride from Baltimore to Box Horn Farm brought back memories of the long-ago trips made in the family Ford. Since it wasn't unusual to pick up rusty nails from a farmer's wagon, nearly every trip meant at least one flat tire. Virginia had always been the first to scramble out of the car. "Let me help," she called. Off came the tire so the inner tube could be removed. Virginia held the tube while her father blew it up with a bicycle pump. Brother John came running with the water can and poured water in a small opening in the tube to find the puncture. If the leak couldn't be patched, a new tube was put in place. Fortunately, Mr. Hall never traveled without two spare inner tubes.

The farm covered 110 acres of hills, dense woods, and a wandering stream. The two-story limestone house had three bedrooms, a library, a large sitting room where the family gathered in the evenings, and a kitchen with a large, inviting table.

Now the farm was a quiet place. John lived in Baltimore with a family of his own. Virginia's father had died three years earlier and her widowed mother lived at the farm by herself. Receiving regular progress reports and not expecting Virginia for another month, Mrs. Hall stood open-mouthed with surprise as a taxi pulled up to the farm and her wayward daughter stepped out. Virginia had come home to heal.

Virginia could not be fitted with an artificial leg until the site of the amputation was completely healed. Though she knew healing would not happen overnight, Virginia was impatient. Waiting was hard.

"No wheelchair," she insisted with her usual stubbornness. "I learned to walk once, and I'll do it again." The more she moved around on crutches, the stronger she became. The stronger she became, the greater distances she could travel. She would not be waited on. Whatever she needed, she got for herself.

Those earlier pain-wracked days may have dimmed her dream a bit, but now it was back in full force. Not one to admit weakness, Virginia was determined to walk again without a crutch or a cane. She would go back to Europe and the consular service. She vowed she would become, just as she had always intended, the nation's first woman diplomat.

As March winds gave way to April rain, Virginia clomped up and down the wooded paths of the farm. Just as she had as a child, she found wounded animals and brought them to her makeshift hospital in the barn. She fixed a splint to the broken leg of a small downy woodpecker. She felt a strong kinship with the beautiful black-and-white bird. She fed orphaned baby rabbits with a milk-filled eye dropper. One morning she found a rabbit with a torn ear. She needed peroxide to clean the wound. The bottle she kept in the barn was empty. Virginia remembered that tobacco was also a good wound healer. She wondered if her late father's tobacco pouch was still in his study. It was. She smiled. He would be glad she was putting it to good use.

Even during those difficult days of recovery, Virginia looked for new enemies to conquer. It was a warm day in late spring when she decided to take on her old nemesis, the cow. It was one of the few defeats she had suffered as a child. No matter how hard she tried, she could not squeeze a single drop of milk out of old Bessie. This time would be different. On crutches, Virginia headed for the barn just before the regular milking time. The farm dogs trotted behind her. Milking time meant a pan of milk set aside for them. Poe, the barn crow, perched on a rafter above.

Virginia plopped herself down in the hot barn, wrinkled her nose at the smell of damp hay, took the milking stool and bucket, and got down to business. Placing her stool at a right angle to the cow, she sat with her head resting on its flank, just the way she'd been taught as a child. She washed the udder with warm water and a clean cloth. She placed a pail under the teats, then squeezed with the top of her thumb and forefinger to force the milk out in a stream. Nothing happened. She squeezed again. Still nothing happened. Determined, she tried again. Not even a drop.

"Give it up, you no-good, turned-up turd!" she yelled at the cow. She wiped rivers of sweat from her face and tried again. This time the warm milk came out in a steady stream and continued until the pail was full. "It's about time," she muttered.

Grinning from ear to ear, Virginia had known from the start who would win. Little did she know, her new milking skill might one day save her life.

At last the day came when the stump was healed enough for Virginia to be fitted with her new leg. She pulled a soft sock over the stump to keep the wooden leg from rubbing and causing blisters. She attached the leg with straps that went around her thigh and waist. The wooden foot moved just as if it were attached to a real ankle. Keeping her sense of humor, she took a long look at the cumbersome new foot and named it Cuthbert.

Learning to walk again was hard work. Virginia fell often, refusing help as she picked herself up. Many days saw little progress.

"I can do this," she yelled, gritting her teeth as she picked herself up for the third time.

She ignored the advice of the physical therapist and spent more time practicing with the artificial leg than was prudent. She lay awake many painful nights with a throbbing, overworked stump.

Woodland paths were the best place to walk. The leaf-covered ground was softer to fall on, and only the spotted deer and striped raccoons were there to see her fall. Finally, the hard work paid off. By the end of May, she walked with only a cane for support. Friends who drove out from Baltimore were astonished to find a smiling and lively Dindy walking without help.

"Of course I'm going back to Europe," she told them. "How else could I become the first woman ambassador? It is just a matter of time. I lost my foot, but not my head."

Virginia knew she was just as capable now as she had ever been. The worst of the pain and suffering were behind her. The bad times in the past would help her to be more understanding of other people's problems.

In September 1934, she threw away the cane. She had spent enough evenings listening to Bob Hope, Jack Benny, and Fred Allen on the radio. It was time to go to work. Europe called. She wrote to Hugh Cumming, assistant secretary of state, advising him that she was ready to resume her consular duties. Could she be sent to Spain? If not, Peru would do. Virginia was never shy about expressing her wishes.

Would the consular service allow her to return? Would they feel the loss of her leg was too much of a handicap? Had her dream become a nightmare? There was no immediate reply to her letter.

CHAPTER 4

The Dream Ends

Day after day, Virginia limped to the mailbox filled with catalogs, circulars, and bills, but no letter from Hugh Cumming. What if all the pain and suffering and hard work had been for nothing? If she couldn't serve her country overseas, what would she do?

The Great Depression years had worsened. There were few jobs to be had. Thousands of people continued to walk the streets, looking for work. Breadlines in every major city fed the hungry. Millions would never regain the savings lost when banks failed. Shut-down businesses had not reopened.

It was on a miserably cold day in late fall that Virginia walked an already snow-covered path to the mailbox. A wet wind whipped her scarf across her face and sent chills up her spine. She flipped open the box and there, among the usual circulars and bills, was an official-looking letter. With a sense of having been through this before, she ignored the rest of the mail and ripped open the envelope. YES! Hugh Cumming wrote they looked forward to her return. At this time, there were no openings at the consulates in Spain or Peru, but there was an opening in Venice, Italy. Did Virginia want the assignment?

"Absolutely!" Virginia replied. She packed her belongings and bought a ticket on the first ship sailing to Europe. She moved so quickly, she crossed the ocean almost before Hugh Cumming had a chance to open her acceptance letter.

"What a difference," Virginia exclaimed as she arrived at the American consulate in Venice. "In Smyrna, even paperclips were hard to come by," she told a coworker.

Here, she was greeted by an impressive building that had recently been redecorated. Elegant tables waxed to a heavy shine held vases of fresh flowers. Rich leather chairs had hand-carved legs and deep red velvet cushions. A Persian rug in soft shades of beige and rose greeted visitors. Polished walnut desks held new typewriters, not at all like the old Remington in Smyrna.

The consulate was a beehive of activity. There were staff members for every task. While Virginia was first assigned the familiar typing and clerical duties, she proved to be so hardworking and capable that Consul General Terry Stewart gave her work with passports and other documents, which was the type of job usually assigned to Foreign Service officers.

For the next four years, Virginia worked at the American consulate in Venice, the city built on water and connected by 150 canals. It was the city known for the legacy of Marco Polo, Tintoretto, and Vivaldi. And now, it was also where the M.S. Milwaukee rested in the harbor, flying the Nazi flag.

One of the rules in the consular service stated that, after five years of service and with good recommendations from superiors, a candidate could take an oral rather than a written examination to become a career Foreign Service officer. By 1937, Virginia had been with the consular service six years. She requested that she be given the oral examination. The reply she received was unbelievable.

She was stunned to read the answer was NO! It would be useless for her to take the examination. The letter said there were no women Foreign Service officers. The message continued, "Any amputation of any portion of a limb or resection of a joint is cause for rejection in the diplomatic career field." An addendum noted that a clerical job had just opened up in a city on the northern coast of Estonia on the Gulf of Finland. Did she want the job?

Virginia was furious. "They amputated my leg," she shouted, "not my head!"

Not one to take no for an answer, Virginia flew to her desk, tossed aside papers, and began typing. She typed letters to senators, representatives, the head of the

Foreign Service, and to the president of the United States. Most of her letters were ignored. The few replies she received pointed out that rules were rules and nothing could be done.

In June 1938, an angry and discouraged Virginia arrived in Tallin, Estonia, where she worked for the next eleven months. She could not know that, within two years, Tallin would be conquered and occupied first by Nazi Germany and then by the Russians, and many of the friends and coworkers she met there would end up in concentration camps.

Her duties were dull and boring. The day came when she had enough of typing letters and memos and filing papers that were never looked at. Where was the future for which she had worked so hard?

"Not in Tallin," she told the consul general. "There has to be more to life than filing papers." She put one last sheet in her typewriter. She typed her letter of resignation. She packed her few belongings and headed for the train station where she bought a ticket for Paris, a city she had always loved. It was a city where she could work as a part-time journalist and take her time deciding what to do next. It was also a city on the brink of war.

DURING THIS TIME IN THE WORLD

1939–1940 German Might Grows

By May 1939, Hitler's power knew no bounds. German Jews were gathered up by the thousands and sent to concentration camps. Jews who realized there was no hope for them in Germany, and who could afford to leave the country, flooded foreign consulates for visas. However, few countries accepted them.

On September 1, 1939, the flames of war were lit when the German army marched through Poland. Tiny Poland could not defend itself against the might of the German army. Surrender came in twenty-six days and the Polish people suffered greatly.

Two days after Germany invaded Poland, Great Britain and France declared war on Germany. The French were confident they could keep the German forces from invading France. For the past four years they had been hard at work building the Maginot line, a thick concrete fortress that covered 180 miles of the German/French border. The line was fortified with heavy guns and there were railways to move troops from one part of the line to another. No stronger defense had ever been built.

In early 1940, Denmark, Norway, Belgium, Luxembourg, and the Netherlands fell to the German might. Great Britain and France knew they had to put up a mighty battle or they would find the German army at their doorstep ready to conquer their countries as well. Winston Churchill, prime minister of Great Britain, told his people he had nothing to offer but "blood, toil, tears, and sweat." The people of France had been sure the German army would turn back when it reached the Maginot line. How wrong they were!

CHAPTER 5

Paris Interlude

In May 1939, apartments in Paris were as scarce as feathers on an alligator. Virginia checked into the Hotel Meurice but couldn't afford more than a few nights there. She learned quickly to grab the morning papers and scan the few For Rent ads. Luck was with her. She was knocking on the door of a brownstone with a flat for rent so early that the half-awake landlady was still in her nightclothes.

"Three months in advance and no pets," the woman told her as she led the way up two flights of steps.

"I'll take it," Virginia responded. She didn't need to see the flat to know it was a bargain compared to what she had been paying at the hotel.

There was a small sitting room with dirty gray walls and a worn leather sofa that doubled as a bed. A chair with a sagging seat had seen better days, along with a coffee table decorated with a crudely carved heart with lovers' names Virginia couldn't make out. Leaving a window open brought the smell of frying bacon or cooking cabbage from the flats below. Just off the sitting room was a kitchenette with one small burner where she heated water for tea or soup. She washed dishes in a rusty sink with no hot water. Above the sink, she tacked her reminder of home, the photograph of Box Horn Farm.

The ugly flat reminded Virginia that she was not on a Paris holiday. To pay the rent and buy her food, she needed a job. She contacted friends of her late father at several American newspapers. With all of Europe in an upheaval, could they use a freelance journalist? "Absolutely!" three editors replied. "Send us all you've got."

Every day Virginia walked the streets, eyes and ears alert for firsthand stories. She found the streets flooded with Jewish refugees from Hitler's Germany. Most had escaped with only the shirts on their backs, and few could find work. Jobs went to French citizens who, remembering World War I, had little use for the refugees. Jewish physicians and college professors alike became street sweepers.

The weeks of summer passed. Virginia fell into a routine. She bought a secondhand bicycle, and early mornings she biked to the open-air market to purchase milk, potatoes, fresh-baked bread, and sometimes a plump chicken for her evening meal. Her next stop was the newspaper kiosk for the French, German, and Italian papers.

"LOOK OUT!" The basket on Virginia's bike was so full, she saw the woman only at the last minute. She jerked the wheel sharply to the left, but too late! Bike, basket, and Virginia came tumbling to the sidewalk, a mass of arms, legs, newspapers, and food.

"Are you hurt?"

Virginia looked up to see a pretty young woman with curly red hair, wide blue eyes, a gentle mouth, and a dimpled chin. She stood the bike upright and bent down to gather the foodstuffs and papers that had scattered in all directions.

"Only thing hurt is my pride," Virginia said, grinning sheepishly and pulling herself up. "It was my own stupid fault for not watching where I was going."

"Do you read all these?" The woman pointed to the French and German newspapers.

"It's my job," Virginia replied. "I send news to papers in the States as a freelance journalist. That's a fancy way of saying I don't have a regular job."

As they talked, the two walked side by side and were surprised when they both stopped at the same brownstone, discovering they were neighbors. Claire de La Tour lived in a first floor flat just below Virginia's. In the lazy summer days that followed, Virginia and Claire became good friends.

On September 3, 1939, the quiet, peaceful days came

to an end. On this hot September day, it was more than 100 degrees in the flat. Virginia stepped out on her small balcony to catch a breath of air when she heard the excited shouts of a paper boy on the street below. France had declared war against Germany. She ran down to the street to grab a paper.

"*C'EST LA GUERRE! C'EST LA GUERRE!*" The war has come! Virginia studied the faces gathered around the newsboy. An old woman crossed herself. Perhaps she had lost loved ones in the First World War. A young mother picked up her two-year-old and clutched him to her as if the threat of danger was imminent. Her face reflected the fear of many around her. Three young men linked arms and danced in the street. If Germany attempted to invade France, they would be fighting at the Maginot line. They would be a part of the great French army that would send the Germans running back home.

"A second world war," Virginia murmured to herself. "The United States can't avoid this one. There has to be a place for me now."

She returned to her flat and her small writing desk. Her letter to the US State Department told of her experience overseas. She knew France. She spoke the language like a native. It was quite possible the Germans would soon occupy France. Virginia could use her eyes and ears to supply vital information. She asked to become a foreign agent for her country. She could be of invaluable service.

Down the stairs she went and climbed on her bicycle. She arrived at the American embassy in record time, where she handed her letter to an undersecretary. "At last I can be of real service," she said.

The undersecretary shook his head. "Sorry," he told her. "Only official dispatches travel to the United States by courier. You will have to use the regular postal service to send your letter."

"IMBECILE!" A furious Virginia snatched her letter from his hand, turned her back on the undersecretary, and left as quickly as she had come. Mumbling angry words, she biked the eight blocks to the post office, ignoring the friendly waves of shopkeepers she passed. She reached the post office, where she rented a box. Thieves had been looting mailboxes in the flats. She wanted to be sure of a reply. She added the box number to her return address and dropped her letter in the mail. She knew it could be weeks before she got a reply.

Every day, Virginia rode her bicycle from her small flat through the streets of Paris to the post office. Her route took her past a small park where young and old came to escape the heat from their flats and enjoy the green oasis at the edge of the busy city. Small children played hide-and-seek in the bushes. Young mothers pushed baby carriages with their tops up to shield the babies from the hot sun. One mother slapped the hand of her five-year-old as the child reached down to pick a brightly colored tulip in a flowerbed by a small fountain.

"Anything today?" Claire asked as Virginia returned to the flat. The answer day after day was NO!

Weeks passed. The bicycle lady was a familiar sight to the old men who sat on the same benches every day, gossiping and soaking in the sunshine. They called out greetings. Virginia gave a friendly wave and cycled on until she reached her destination.

Day after day, disappointment waited. Day after day, the postal box was empty. But finally the day came when the box was not empty. Virginia reached in and pulled out an official-looking letter. At last, a reply!

Hands shaking in excited anticipation, she ripped open the envelope. Whatever she was asked to do, she was ready. No task would be too difficult. No assignment was too dangerous.

"IDIOTS!" she yelled. The words jumped of the page, stinging her eyes like tiny arrows. She could not believe what she was reading.

"*MERDE!*" Her angry shout made heads turn. The letter said she could not serve because she had lost her leg, and because she was a woman. Virginia knew she had not lost her brains. She had not lost her eyes and ears nor her knowledge of languages. She had not lost her determination. She could get around as well as any woman with two good legs. She would NOT BE TOLD NO!

Virginia made up her mind. "If I cannot serve my country, I will serve France!"

CHAPTER 6

Virginia Goes to War

Virginia wasted no time. Claire had mentioned an organization that needed volunteers badly. It did not matter if they were women; it did not matter if they were handicapped. Virginia did not return to her flat. She biked directly to the building where the office of the Services Sanitaires de l'Armée was located. Along the way, she passed a line of young men waiting to enlist in the French army. Young boys trying to look old enough to serve their country joked with each other about how they would run the Germans back to the Rhine if they tried to invade France. Virginia smiled at the eager recruits. Some were using the backs of others to fill out papers handed to them by a smiling young woman. Virginia waved, and two laughing boys waved back.

After climbing three flights of stairs and reading signs on a half-dozen doors, Virginia found the office she was seeking. A harried-looking woman sat behind a large oak desk buried under paperwork. She flipped a gray strand of hair out of her tired eyes and looked over her glasses at the approaching young woman.

Virginia spoke with a quiet, controlled firmness. "I'll go anywhere you ask and do any job you give me if it helps to keep the Germans out of France."

"Is that so?" the woman asked as she brushed aside the stack of papers. She pushed her glasses up to get a better look at this brash young woman. The set of Virginia's jaw and the flash of her eyes told her this was a determined recruit. The outspoken newcomer who stood before her could be very useful despite the wooden leg she made no attempt to hide. For a moment the woman did not reply.

"Can you drive a truck?" she asked. "The ambulance service needs drivers."

Virginia nodded yes. She had never driven a truck, but she could drive a car. There couldn't be much difference.

"Can you use another driver?" Virginia asked, thinking of Claire. "I know someone else eager to volunteer."

She was right. With little ceremony, Virginia and Claire enlisted in the Services Sanitaires de l'Armée and, after four weeks of training, became privates second class.

A month of slapping bandages on pretend wounds and executing self-defense moves against an invisible enemy was followed by four months in Paris, doing nothing. Rations were short. The open-air markets were closed. Both heat and food were hard to come by. The inactivity was getting to Virginia; she was about ready to resign when orders finally came. She and Claire were to report to Metz on the Western Front. There they were to join a medical unit consisting of eight trucks and twelve drivers. In addition to first aid, every driver had taken a crash course in mechanics. It was a needed course. Some of the ambulances were the very old Deux Chevauxs used in World War I.

The trip to Metz was made in twilight with no lights because the region was still under shell fire. They traveled a narrow road scattered with craters left by bombs. Scorched earth led to the barracks that housed the ambulance service. There they were given bread and cheese, a thin blanket, and a straw pallet for a bed. The straw turned out to be a luxury, for in the coming days what little sleep was possible was done inside the ambulance, on the ground, or in open fields.

There was no time to settle in as an urgent call came in for drivers.

"Pick up two badly wounded men at the battlefield aid station," they were ordered by the dispatcher. The aid station was located not more than 300 yards from the fighting. After a few false starts, Virginia drove the ambulance in the pitch-black night, without lights, over roads that were pockmarked from shells, moving as quickly as she dared.

One of the wounded, a young boy, had been hit in the chest. As Virginia and Claire lifted his stretcher into the ambulance, he looked at Virginia with sad, tired eyes and gave a brave smile. By the time of their arrival in Metz, he had given up his life.

The hospital at Metz was a convent where every room but one had been hit by a shell. The corridors were used as wards where many of the wounded suffered through, for there were no drugs to give them. Food was scarce. The one meal a day was thin potato soup. Bandages were nonexistent. Clothing of the dead was ripped up to make bandages for the living.

There were times when an assignment meant meeting trains bringing in the wounded. On one moonlit night, Virginia and Claire waited at a small railway station where they were assigned to meet another troop train. Their job was to move the wounded to a freight shed set up as a makeshift hospital.

In the distance, they heard the crash of artillery. Enemy planes buzzed overhead. The ambulance crews worked in a blackout. The train pulled in without lights, and Virginia and the other drivers moved quickly in the dark, carrying the wounded soldiers from the train to the freight shed.

On the third trip, the drivers were met by a doctor who signaled them to stop. The freight shed was overflowing with wounded. There was no room for more. Incoming wounded would have to be transported to another field hospital. Each ambulance turned around and set off traveling in the dark. The smallest light was a target for an enemy plane. Virginia drove through the black night, safely delivering her wounded to a small chateau high up on a hill. Once there, the injured men were placed on beds of straw, in long rows. An exhausted doctor moved from patient to patient, doing what he could. Local women served as nurses, bathing fevered faces and changing dressings. Virginia and Claire made four more trips that night.

Morning found Claire sleeping on an empty stretcher and an exhausted Virginia half-asleep in the empty train station, eyes closed, her back propped up against a packing crate. She was in that drowsy state of being half-awake when, without warning, something cold slid across her hand.

Cautiously, she reached for anything she could use as a weapon. Her hand closed around a heavy stick. She sat up suddenly, ready to hit her attacker. One quick look and Virginia burst out laughing. A small white dog, a tiny walking dust mop, threw its front legs and paws around her neck and licked her face with enthusiasm.

"Hey, pup, where did you come from?" she asked with a smile. The friendly stray, part terrier and part mutt, was dirty and hungry. Virginia reached for her field rations and held out a crust of bread. It disappeared in one gulp. Virginia tore off another piece and another. The happy pup curled up on her lap and buried its head under her arm. When the drivers were called back to duty, the pup followed, keeping pace with its new mistress.

Virginia reached her ambulance, banged on the rear door to awaken Claire, and climbed into the driver's seat. The dog hopped up beside her. From that day on, Mop became a familiar sight at the train stations and rear areas. The pup and Virginia traveled together for the four months she drove the ambulance. By now, all of the drivers knew Mop was her good luck charm. In all the time Mop traveled with Virginia and Claire, their ambulance took not a single hit by fire from the German guns or planes.

By June 1940, the fighting in France was over. On June 22, France signed an armistice with Germany. A victorious German army marched into a stunned Paris with all its military might.

In the once-glorious city, German troops were everywhere. The French flags came down. From the Eiffel Tower flew the hated German swastika. Virginia and Claire were told they were no longer needed as ambulance drivers. As privates in the ambulance service, they were subject to capture. They should leave the area immediately.

"We'll go to my home in Cahors," Claire told Virginia. "It's a long journey south but Cahors is an unoccupied area." Virginia agreed that safety, at least temporarily, was in Cahors. It was a great distance, especially when they had no transportation: 857 kilometers or about 500 miles.

Chaos reigned in the ambulance compound. Meals were left untouched. Belongings were shoved roughly into knapsacks. Insignias were painted over on some of the ambulances that would serve as escape vehicles. Uniforms were shed, but unfortunately uniforms were the only clothing the two women had.

"What luck," Claire said as she spotted a troop transport with the motor running. "Hold up," she yelled to the driver. "Are you going south? Can we hitch a ride?"

A sharp bark caught Virginia's attention. She reached down and rubbed Mop's chin. "Did you think we had forgotten you?" she asked. "Not on your life. You're coming with us."

Mop's tail wagged furiously as Virginia gathered the pup in her arms.

The women slept nearly five hours and awoke when the truck made an abrupt stop in farm country just outside Paris. They waved their thanks as the transport continued west. Now they had to find a ride south to Cahors, still a distance of 575 kilometers.

"We need to shed these uniforms," Virginia told Claire. Claire agreed.

Traveling on foot, they passed several small farms. Behind one stone cottage, Virginia spotted worn and tattered clothing flapping in the wind on a makeshift clothesline. They made their way up a stone path to the rough oak door, wrinkling their noses at the hearty odor of manure and chimney smoke.

A round-cheeked, heavyset woman answered their knock, her shrewd eyes taking in the situation at once. She knew if these brave women still in uniform were captured, they would be at the mercy of the hated Germans. "Yes," she could provide clothing. "Come in, come in," she said.

Madame Long, a widow, farmed with her son the few acres of land they owned, but this year the fields lay bare. The Germans were taking all of the crops; and the Longs, like many other farmers, refused to plant anything that would feed the invaders.

The little woman sat Virginia and Claire down at a plain but clean wooden table. She hung the kettle over a fireplace with bricks heavily coated with years of soot. She laid out a meal of fresh-baked bread and cheese, poured tea, then climbed a dark staircase to search for clothes. In moments, she reappeared, her short arms loaded with skirts and tops. Virginia and Claire were quickly transformed from uniformed privates into ordinary farm girls with simple well-worn shirts, long cotton skirts, and coarse brown aprons.

"You need rest," Madame Long observed. "I've an extra bed if you want to stay the night."

As tempting as the offer was, the two knew it was best not to linger, especially this close to Paris, where Germans were everywhere. Thanking Madame Long for her kindness, they resumed their journey south on foot.

For some of the distance, they were able to hitch rides on slow and bumpy farmers' carts pulled by half-starved horses. Nights were spent in the open or in deserted barns. Dirty and exhausted, they arrived safely in Cahors four days later.

Claire was amazed to see her father's butcher shop still open, not only because of the shortage of meat, but because of the hostile climate throughout France toward Jews. Claire's family was Jewish. While Cahors was not yet part of occupied France, they knew it soon would be. Claire's family made plans to move much farther south to a farm near Carcasserone, owned by distant cousins. They would be leaving within the week.

"You must travel with us," Claire begged Virginia.

Virginia remained with the de La Tours until their

departure. The week of rest gave time for her blistered stump to begin healing. The driving, the constant dampness, and the heavy lifting had taken their toll. Until she was completely healed, it was impossible for her to walk without a limp.

In Cahors, Virginia heard a call for ambulance drivers to move the wounded in an area near Paris. Leaving Mop in Claire's loving care, Virginia hitched a ride north with a friendly farmer. The work lasted only six weeks.

Virginia thought long and hard about what to do next. She knew she could be useful in the fight against the Germans. Her own country had turned her down as a spy. Perhaps she might have better luck with the British. It was time, Virginia decided, to go to England.

The heat of the Paris train station was sweltering. Virginia had shed her ambulance driver's uniform for the trim green suit and long-sleeved white blouse provided by Claire. Her one foot, swollen from the damp boots the ambulance drivers wore, made getting on a shoe difficult.

In the crowded, noisy station, platforms were heaped with boxes and cartons and luggage. Porters shouted over the noise of bells and whistles and the hiss of steam from arriving and departing trains. The smell of smoke lay over the tracks. Virginia waited in a long line to present her passport to the German guard. First he looked at the picture on the passport. Then he looked at Virginia. After grueling months with the ambulance service, Virginia knew she looked much older than the passport picture. Finally, the guard handed her the passport with a nod, and she boarded the train for Spain.

From there she booked passage on a ship to London. If her own country could not use her knowledge of French and German and her willingness to do anything to stop the Nazis, then perhaps Great Britain could. Little did Virginia know that, when she finally reached London, she would begin a whole new life as a SUPER SPY!

DURING THIS TIME IN THE WORLD

1940–1941 Occupied France

On June 22, 1940, a defeated France signed an armistice with Germany. The Germans would control Northern and Western France and the Atlantic Coast. The French government in the tiny town of Vichy would be responsible for Southern France; but the French leader, Marshal Pétain, a man in his eighties, would still take orders from the Germans.

To escape the German occupation, thousands of young Frenchmen made their way to North Africa and Great Britain to continue the fight. Others remained in France to become Resistance fighters of the French Underground.

Armistice terms set forth by the Germans included:

- No photographs of any kind could be taken outdoors.
- No one could own a radio, take part in a parade, or fly a flag.
- No one could appear on the streets between 11:00 p.m. and 6:00 a.m.
- A pass was needed, and very difficult to get, to travel south to unoccupied territory.

The French army was disbanded, and one-and-a-half-million French soldiers, captured by the Germans, remained prisoners of war. In addition, France had to pay the occupation costs, and eighty percent of all crops and farm goods produced went to feed the German troops.

At this same time, Great Britain set up an organization known as the Special Operations Executive (SOE), which was, in truth, an agency formed to train spies and send them to France and other areas where vital information was needed.

CHAPTER 7

The Making of a Spy

Maurice Buckmaster's stomach curled into a knot as he gazed at the large map on the wall. It showed the five tiny defenseless countries the German army had rolled over like a massive tsunami wave. It was September 1940. The brave French forces had also fallen under the might of the invaders. Buckmaster, head of London's Special Operations Executive, French section, shivered. Would Great Britain be next?

Power-hungry Hitler was out to rule not only Germany, but the entire world. Would anyone be able to stop this madman? Buckmaster was desperate to find out what the Germans in France were planning. He needed answers and he needed them now. Only a master spy could get these answers for him.

He flipped open a folder on his desk sent to him by Vera Atkins, a trusted agent. Clipped to the folder was a photograph of a young woman with a most determined chin. Her dark hair fell in soft waves around her narrow face. She was unsmiling, yet her direct gaze left the impression she was the guardian of a great secret. The folder revealed an adventurous woman who had been well-educated at prestigious Radcliffe College and Barnard College (Columbia University), had worked in US embassies all over Europe, spoke four languages, and who had lived in France and knew the language and the people well. Her name was Virginia Hall, a woman who seemed to greet every new assignment as a welcome challenge. Here might be the answer Buckmaster was seeking. Virginia Hall could well be the ideal spy.

Buckmaster was amazed when her file revealed that this American woman had recently returned from driving an ambulance on the front lines in France. In uniform she could have been captured by the Germans and made a prisoner of war. She escaped just after the invaders reached Paris and was now working in the code room of the American embassy.

"Set up a lunch meeting with Virginia Hall," Buckmaster told Atkins.

The following day, the thirty-four-year-old woman entered the small cafe where Buckmaster waited. With a shock he realized he had not read the entire folder. He was startled to see this woman who craved adventure and laughed at danger had a wooden leg.

Despite Buckmaster's misgivings, the interview went well. Virginia gave no-nonsense answers to the spy chief's questions. She looked at him directly with eyes both shrewd and intelligent.

"I expect to be given the same work as my male counterparts," she told Buckmaster. "No accommodation is needed."

Buckmaster nodded. What he had in mind was to give Virginia the work of a master spy!

"You'll be working for the SOE. The training program is not for the faint of heart," he told her. "If you successfully complete the training, you will be sent to France. While there, you will keep your eyes and ears open, and coordinate and distribute funds to the many small, fragmented Resistance groups. You will assist escaped prisoners of war and downed pilots with clothing, food, shelter, false identity cards, and guides to take them across the demarcation line to the south of France."

Buckmaster looked Virginia in the eye. "It is a dangerous job. The Gestapo has eyes and ears everywhere. If you are caught, you will be shot."

Virginia nodded. "Who would suspect a spy with a wooden leg?" She laughed. "When do I start?"

In February 1941, Virginia quit her embassy job and began training outside London at Wanborough Manor, where she was told, "Your code name is Germaine."

At the end of the day with orders given only in French, and with every muscle screaming for mercy, an exhausted Virginia sank gratefully to her bunk. Her whole body ached, but especially the stump of her injured leg. With stiff fingers, she removed the harness that attached her false foot. The stump was an angry red. Physical training, including long uphill hikes, was tough, but Virginia kept up despite her wooden leg. She was careful to keep the stump covered with a clean sock; still, some rubbing and irritation could not be avoided.

As she massaged the stump with her left hand, she practiced tapping out Morse code with the right against the metal frame of the bunk. Not one minute of training was wasted.

Learning Morse code was essential, as was learning to handle weapons, including guns, knives, and explosives. There was even training at mealtimes. Americans could quickly give themselves away by holding a fork in the right hand.

"Hello, my name is Michelle. What's yours?" The English speaker was a young woman, slender and small with a tangled mass of brown hair. Her mouth turned up at the corners as she smiled at Virginia. She pulled a large duffel bag through the door.

Another test? Virginia wondered. She could not recall seeing the woman before. She directed a steady gaze at her, but said nothing. Friendships among recruits at Wanborough were forbidden as was any talk about past lives or activities. If conversation got too personal,

Virginia fixed her dark-eyed gaze on the person in question and changed the subject in a voice that carried the ring of authority. She motioned to a bunk by the door. "That one's empty," she said in French.

Agents sent to France had to speak fluent French and be so familiar with the country that they could pass for French people. A poor accent, lack of knowledge of the countryside, or even looking the wrong way before crossing the street could give an agent away. Capture meant a firing squad. Virginia followed the training rules to the letter. She did not intend to face a firing squad, not in France nor anywhere else.

Late one afternoon, three weeks into training, the recruits returned to their barracks to find sealed envelopes on their bunks. The notices had been issued. A few of the recruits would continue training in Scotland. Others would be sent home.

Virginia picked up her envelope. Surely, she would not be sent home. Surely, she would not face rejection again. A burst of adrenalin flowed through her veins as she pushed back the clasp on the brown envelope and removed a single sheet of paper.

YES! She was accepted for more rigorous training in Scotland. However, understanding the danger, if she wished to return to London at this point, she could do so without censure.

"Scotland, it is," Virginia said, wrinkling her smooth brow. "Lord knows what's in store now!"

She soon found out. In Scotland, both the physical and mental training intensified. She was part of raiding parties and demolition teams. She set up escape routes and learned to silently ward off an attacker. She led groups on raids through small towns with wide and quiet streets, keeping in the shadow of thick shrubs and shady elms.

Late one night, following a day of rigorous training, the door to her sleeping quarters smashed open. Strong hands pulled Virginia from her cot. "YOUR NAME! YOUR NAME! AT ONCE!" a screaming enemy shouted, the veins on his neck pumping in and out as though about to burst. He grabbed a straight chair and dragged Virginia toward it, at the same time pushing his face so close to hers, she could feel the spit from his mouth. She bit back a moan as her arms were whipped behind her and rough ropes bound her wrists.

"NAME? MISSION? CONTACTS?" the red-faced interrogator screamed.

She felt the sting of a black leather glove on her face and arms. She felt a trickle of blood as the sharp point of a long-handled knife pricked her neck. It became near to impossible to remain silent as more and more information was demanded. Virginia sat up straight. She had gone through worse than this. She would not break. She gazed at her attacker, her eyes artless and serene, and did not utter a sound.

After a full night of interrogation, she rubbed her aching wrists as her bonds were released. Her attacker left as silently as he had entered. She sank down on her waiting cot, but rest was not to be. "Germaine! Report to HQ," a voice called from the hallway.

Reaching headquarters, she was ordered to lead a mock commando raid on the enemy. As a gray haze hung over the valley, an exhausted Virginia pulled herself together and led her silent team over a three-mile terrain along steep paths, wet and full of roots, to the designated target, all the time dodging the enemy waiting to capture her team.

"Well done, Germaine," was the brisk comment from her training officer.

Three weeks later, another notice was tossed on her cot. She passed her training with flying colors and was ordered to return to London for a final meeting with Buckmaster.

It was a tougher, stronger Virginia who faced Buckmaster this time.

"Arrangements have been made with the *New York Post* to use you as a roving correspondent," he told her. "You will travel by ship to Lisbon and by train from there to Vichy. You must register your credentials with the American embassy in Lyons and with the Vichy police, as all foreigners are required to do. Good luck!"

Virginia would need much more than luck to evade the long-reaching clutches of the Gestapo.

CHAPTER 8

Code Name Germaine

In late August 1941, Vichy was not only the Hot Springs of France, it had become the hot spot of France. Controlled by the Nazis, Vichy was the center of police activity. It was the city where spies were unmasked and put to death.

Virginia Hall was a spy!

As an American journalist, Virginia found lodging in an inexpensive hotel on Rue Jardet. Strapped around her waist were one million bogus francs to be used by the Underground to purchase food and weapons. She dared not leave the money in her room because Gestapo agents made routine searches of hotel rooms.

Her instructions were to meet immediately with Jacques, a French agent. She memorized the time and date. The meeting place, a small cafe, was within walking distance from her hotel. She set out in the early evening, passing few people. There was none of the cheerful chatter she remembered from past years.

A weather-beaten sign pointed to steps that led down to the cafe. A bell rang over the door as she entered the overcrowded room hazy with cigarette smoke. Searching the faces of the diners, Virginia had no trouble finding Jacques. Shabby boots, frayed jacket, cap pulled over one eye, he struck a relaxed pose at a far table, his back against a wall. His face was lean and lanky with a two-day-old beard. He appeared to pay no attention to Virginia nor to anyone around him, yet Virginia knew he was aware of every person in the cafe. He sat with a clear view of the door and gave a faint nod as Virginia entered. Without hesitating, she approached his table. He motioned her to sit.

"It is not possible to do the work you have been sent to do in Vichy," he told her. "You can operate with less danger in Lyons. Unlike Vichy, there is a small Underground group there who can assist you. When you arrive, contact Dr. Jean Rousset who will put you in touch with Resistance leaders and others who will provide trucks to move supplies from parachute drops, and still others who operate safe houses."

Virginia said little but nodded her understanding. "Good luck," Jacques clasped one of her hands in both of his, gave it a hearty squeeze, and disappeared through the smoky haze.

In the few days she spent in the city, Virginia found the people of Vichy to be wary of strangers and resentful of the police, whose orders came from the Germans.

Clothing was so scarce as to be almost nonexistent, and there was strict rationing of food. Before making the trip to Lyons, Virginia sent off her first article as a *Post* correspondent.

> I received my ration card for the month of September today. As I understand it I am allowed ten ounces of bread per day. Beyond that, my allotments for the month are as follows: 2 ounces of cheese, 25 ounces of fats, 20 ounces of sugar, 10 ounces of meat, and 6 ounces of coffee. And by coffee they mean 2 ounces of real coffee and 4 ounces of some kind of substitute material. No rice, noodles, or chocolate are available during the month of September as these are reserved for colder months. France would be a paradise for a vegetarian if there was milk, cheese, and butter; but I haven't seen any butter, and there is no milk.

After less than a week in Vichy, Virginia moved 123 miles away to Lyons, a city of great cathedrals and fifteenth-century mansions built by the silk barons of earlier times. Again, she found rooms in a small hotel, a former mansion which still boasted *traboules* or secret passages, which could serve as escape routes in case of Gestapo raids.

But more safe houses and escape routes were needed because informers—of whom there were many—would soon make the Gestapo aware of the existence of the *traboules*.

Virginia purchased a rusty bike and set out to explore the city. She rode past factories at the edges of the city and past broad streets and fine lawns leading to homes of the wealthy. Two rivers flowed through the town and high on a hill above the point where the rivers met, Virginia found what she was seeking: a convent.

She walked her bicycle up the hill and reached for the brass bell pull beside a pair of massive wooden doors. After a short time, she heard footsteps as an elderly sister bustled to the door, her wooden beads clicking.

"Please," the nun invited, "come in." She was a small, plump woman with deep brown eyes, a smooth brow, and a kindly mouth. Her black habit fit tightly around her face.

She led the way down a narrow hall, past windows of stained glass to a sitting room all clean and fresh with delicate furniture and blue velvet draperies tied back on either side of a polished window. "I am Sister Agnes," she said. "How can I help you?"

Virginia instinctively knew this little round woman could be trusted. She learned that the convent was a haven for wealthy women who could afford a large one-time payment to escape the outside world. The convent was also a school where the sisters boarded and taught girls from wealthy families.

Virginia explained her mission. "This is the last place the Germans will look for an escaped prisoner or British flyer," she told Sister Agnes.

Without hesitation, the nun agreed and was given a password that would be used to admit, from time to time, one or more unexpected guests.

The convent had one small problem, however. If they were to shelter British airmen and escaped prisoners, they would need to feed them. Food was scarce. Even the convent garden was raided by the enemy. Everything was bought with supply coupons issued by the Germans.

With dozens of downed flyers roaming through France, Virginia would meet the problem again and again. It was time to call on the Catins, an elderly husband and wife who faithfully served the Resistance in many ways. Jacques had nicknamed them the "coupon couple." To obtain the needed coupons, they visited smaller villages where the overweight, red-faced Monsieur Catin would fake a heart attack just outside the town hall door. As people rushed to his aid, tiny, fluttery

Madame Catin, in pretending to search for a cup for water, rifled through everything she could find: tickets, coupons, stamps, identity cards. The most insignificant document could prove useful. If questioned, the white-haired lady scrunched up her wrinkled face, looking lost and confused. Virginia sought them out at once.

"Yes," the Catins told Virginia. They had food coupons from a recent raid on the Avignon Town Hall. They would deliver them to Sister Agnes at the convent.

"Perhaps there could be an extra benefit," the cheerful Madame Catin joked. "She can pray that our next raid is as successful as the last."

In her next report two weeks later to Buckmaster, Virginia explained: "I've moved to Lyons, which is a much better idea. I can go and see things from here, travel being slightly less horrible than from Vichy. And I've made a lot of friends—doctors, businessmen, a few newspaper people (they are so daft, I don't like them, though), refugees, professors. One nice red-headed doctor has a *chassé* nearby, so I'm going shooting again. I shall keep Cuthbert well out of the way."

In Vichy, it had been difficult to tell a collaborator from one loyal to the Resistance. The task proved to be easier in Lyons.

Here, following Jacques's advice, Virginia found loyal Frenchmen like big, lumbering Monsieur Labourier who had his trucks ready at the air drops. There he would use his massive arms to load heavy weapons and hide them back in his warehouse.

The need for money was constant with the Resistance network—for weapons, travel, lodging, clothing, and supplies. When Virginia arrived, one million counterfeit francs were to be distributed to Resistance networks as needed, but the money also had to be accounted for.

"I don't have time to be a bookkeeper," Virginia grumbled, untying a money belt from around her waist. She and Monsieur Labourier had just returned to his warehouse from an airdrop.

Monsieur Labourier put his massive head back and roared with laughter. "Such a problem to have! What to do with one million francs? We should all have such a problem! Do not worry," he told Virginia, "I am very good at figures. I will be your treasurer."

Virginia was relieved. There was no doubt this big bear of a man, his belly bouncing with hearty laughter, could be trusted to act as treasurer, keeping careful records of the money Virginia would distribute.

Another of Virginia's valuable contacts was Madame Germaine Guérin, a clever woman who provided more safe houses. While Virginia knew that close friendships were to be avoided, it was difficult not to feel a special closeness with Madame Guérin. She was a handsome woman with thick black hair, a square face, and soft gray eyes. Her voice was hoarse, her laughter loud. Pleasant of both face and disposition, she asked no questions but accepted Virginia on blind faith.

"I have friends and I have money," she told Virginia. "What better use to make of both than to help the Resistance?" Without hesitation, she used her many contacts and her own money to locate and rent flats in out-of-the-way places. Amazingly, she supplied the flats with heating stoves and coal, both extremely hard to find.

CHAPTER 9

The Resistance

When not cycling the countryside to find fields that would make ideal airdrops, Virginia made the rounds of smelly bistros and smoky restaurants. Once there, she perched on a barstool next to an unsuspecting young soldier and struck up a conversation. She reminded the Germans of their sisters at home. Those men who talked freely to her never suspected that the woman with soft brown hair and twinkling eyes was a spy. The information about troop movements and supplies was easy to gather. Getting it to London was not easy at all. The radio operators Virginia used moved frequently to avoid German direction finders. Some operators were as far away as Avignon. To get messages back and forth, reliable couriers were needed.

"Why weren't we trained as radio operators?" Virginia complained to Madame Catin, handing her a coded message. "Then there would be no need for all this running back and forth."

Virginia helped the elderly Catins on with their coats. No one suspected the feeble couple who needed assistance boarding the train to be risking their lives carrying messages to Avignon to be transmitted to London.

The German noose was getting tighter and tighter by late fall 1941. Orders from General von Stulpnagel, the military governor of Paris, made it clear that death by firing squad would be the punishment for helping downed British flyers.

Virginia received more and more reports of the arrests of Resistance members. New members were needed to take their places, but extreme caution was required in meeting new contacts. It was often difficult to separate the loyal French from the Nazi collaborators. Yet, Virginia possessed an uncanny sixth sense that allowed her to tell the difference. Many times she left a restaurant or bar without making contact, but on this particular evening she immediately greeted the jolly Monsieur and Madame Joulian. So much did they resemble each other, they could have been twins instead of husband and wife. Large of stature, they had soft, plump middle-aged faces with deep wrinkle lines around full lips, the result of many years of laughter.

"We can provide warm welcome and a safe house for the pilots," Madame Joulian told Virginia. Monsieur Joulian, who was a factory owner, offered to give Virginia information about war materials being sent to Germany from France.

Virginia smiled. There was no doubt these two would be valuable additions to the network.

Virginia's days grew busier. She met with Resistance fighters to provide them with weapons and funds to carry out their clandestine missions. She arranged for transmission of vital messages and often took on the dangerous role of courier. She scoured the countryside for suitable drop zones for British Lysanders to parachute containers of weapons, and she arranged transport of the weapons to hiding places. Above all, in every situation, she remained cool and collected.

In stopping the transport of war materials from factories in France to Germany, Virginia did not hesitate to use blackmail. The French arms merchant, Schneider-Cressuet, had been bombed by seventy-five British Lancasters, causing minor damage to the factory, but resulting in the deaths of more than 1,000 French workers.

To prevent such a tragedy from happening again, messages were sent to the Peugeot family whose factory made tank turrets for the German army. The family was given a choice: "Either the RAF [Royal Air Force] will bomb the factory and surrounding residential area, or the machinery will be carefully blown up by members of the French Resistance without damage to the building or injuries to the workers."

The choice was made. The machinery was carefully destroyed, no one was injured, and the supply of tank turrets to Germany was stopped.

Late in November 1941, Virginia was awakened by a soft tapping on her door. It was after 11:00 at night. Madame Joulian stood there, looking worried and wringing her hands. Without a word, she motioned to Virginia that she needed help.

Virginia nodded, "One moment."

She quickly pulled on a heavy cable knit sweater and long wool skirt and boots. Moving quietly down darkened stairs, the two stepped out into a wide and silent street. There was little traffic in this small French village. No voices echoed from porches or balconies. No music came from windows closed against the chill November winds.

"This way," Madame Joulian whispered. She led the way by the light of a frozen moon to a side street. There in the shadows of a boarded up building was a donkey cart filled with straw that covered two men.

Virginia grabbed the reins, leading the donkey and the squeaky-wheeled cart over cobblestone streets to the office of Dr. Rousset. He answered his bell at once.

"Quickly, inside," he said. Pushing aside the straw, the men clambered down. Avoiding capture by the Germans on the back roads for a month, both were gaunt and haggard with bluish growths of beard. Dressed as French peasants, the two were British agents.

"We were dropped by parachute more than thirty miles from our target landing," one man explained. "As soon as we landed, two Frenchmen approached. There was a farmhouse nearby." The man pointed in a wide circle in all directions. "We were surrounded by Germans. The Frenchmen took our chutes and motioned for us to hide in the hedgerows. Then they disappeared. We could hear the Germans approaching on their motorcycles, searching up and down the roads. We remained in the hedgerows for three hours until they left. We have been on the road ever since."

Dropping men or supplies off target was not unexpected since Virginia's network covered more than 2,000 square miles. Without maps or food, these two had taken chances, begging for rides in passing farm wagons. Luck was with them as they managed time and again to avoid capture.

Virginia considered Dr. Rousset to be one of the most valuable members of the Resistance and one who was most helpful to her. He was tall and stately and, despite his authoritative manner, he was one of the kindest men she had ever known. He took care of any Resistance people who became ill. He issued medical certificates for agents so they would not be drafted for work in German factories. He allowed his office to be used as a mail drop for intelligence information. At Virginia's suggestion, he set up a small clinic for the mentally ill, keeping endangered individuals safe under cover.

Safely delivering the two agents to Dr. Rousset's care, Virginia and Madame Joulian bid the good doctor goodnight.

"STOP! YOUR PAPERS!" The words were shouted as Virginia reached for the donkey's bridle. A local gendarme (man-at-arms) approached and held out his hand.

"As you can see, my friend is very ill and needed medical attention," Virginia pointed to Dr. Rousset's sign and handed the man their identity cards. At that moment the light faded in the doctor's window. Madame Joulian moaned and leaned against the cart. Virginia made a great show of helping the poor sick woman into the cart. The gendarme handed back the papers and waved the women on their way.

The next morning found a sleepy Virginia writing yet another article to send to the *Post* as if nothing had happened the night before, for it was essential to protect her journalist cover. She also felt it important that the people at home were made aware of the worsening conditions in France.

"There is much apathy and fear in the country," she wrote. "The French have had the habit of meekly accepting hardship in the past year. They have accepted stricter and stricter rations, less bread, and less wine. They have finally arrived at the state of eating rutabaga for supper, washed down with mineral water. The country folk are turning more and more against the government and more toward the English."

She was pleased to be able to send reports to Buckmaster on the fate of the wandering British agents. "Both men are in good spirits and frightfully pleased at having contacted us, because a month of aimless and seemingly hopeless wandering, without reliable means of obtaining food, has been discouraging, especially having been landed in the wrong place. As to Dr. Rousset, I hope you will give him a large medal some day."

In a follow-up report, Virginia informed Buckmaster, "Somebody has been a dope and has given my name and address away. I am getting an astounding number of people at my door who want to go to England. This can be dangerous for everyone. So I am moving sometime this week to another apartment. The flat is on the sixth floor (no elevator yet) and the name on the door will be J." Then she added, "By the way, if you could ever send me a piece of soap I should be both very happy and much cleaner."

On December 7, 1941, terrible news came over the wireless: "At 7:55 a.m., the Japanese launched an aerial attack against the US Naval base at Pearl Harbor (Hawaii). Damage to ships and planes was heavy. Deaths total more than 2,000."

Virginia stared at the wireless in amazement. All those young lives lost in an unprovoked attack! She pushed aside her half-eaten breakfast. "The US will have to get into the war now," she muttered.

She was right. The United States declared war on Japan on December 8, and three days later, returned declarations of war against Germany and Italy. Virginia, as a US citizen, was now an enemy of the Germans. In her last article as a reporter, she told of the tremendous increase of hungry French citizens stealing food and other necessities. A hungry person does not worry about the law. Ration books were a joke because there was no food to buy. Some Frenchmen who had no jobs signed up to work in factories in Germany. "This might be a good way to get spies into Germany," she wrote Buckmaster. She also wrote, "The German stranglehold is tightening around our throats."

Unfortunately, as a British agent, it could be Virginia's throat destined for the Gestapo noose.

DURING THIS TIME IN THE WORLD

1942–1943 The War Intensifies

With the attack on Pearl Harbor, the American people threw themselves completely into the war effort. Within two years, the armed forces grew in numbers from 160,000 to six million. Aircraft numbering 2,500 at the beginning of 1942 grew to 80,000 aircraft two years later.

In the winter of 1941–42, Germany invaded Russia, but the snow, mud, cold, darkness, and the might of the Russian army pushed the Germans back. In November 1942, British forces successfully drove the Germans from North Africa. The invasion of North Africa brought a flood of German troops into Vichy, creating an occupation force in Southern France. Time was running out. With the arrival of the German troops came the Gestapo, sharp-faced men, sometimes in the black uniform with swastika armbands, sometimes in plain clothes.

It was not only the British agents who were in danger. The Germans were hunting down members of any groups thought to be a danger to them. Those who escaped arrest went into hiding in the mountains and the dense forests. Escaped soldiers from the French army also fled to these hiding places. These freedom fighters joined other Resistance groups to organize attacks on German forces.

CHAPTER 10

ESCAPE!

It was time for Virginia to drop her American reporter disguise and pose as a French woman with two new names, Marie and Philomene. Nights found her in evening dress, chatting with German soldiers in bars and restaurants. The men were grateful to talk about home with this pretty woman who knew their language. "Tell me about your family," she asked, followed by innocent sounding questions, such as, "Do you expect to be here long?" Their answers often provided needed information about troop movements.

The French Resistance forces could not fight without money and weapons. Daylight hours found Virginia riding her rusty bike into the country to find the most level yet secluded spots for landings and parachute drops to get these necessary supplies. In addition to sending military information, Virginia kept Buckmaster informed about the temper of the French people.

She wrote: "People (the French) take a pretty sour view of the British these days, but they are still hoping for their victory and many of them are willing to help, but they would appreciate seeing something concrete besides retreating. They acknowledge the vastness of the task the British have taken on, but are not able to take the really broad view . . . The propaganda of the German showing that the German soldier is shedding his blood to defend France from the Russians is received here with good humor and a great willingness to let them shed as much blood as they like—the more the better, indeed— but it does get through to certain mentalities, and the constant drumming of German propaganda has its effect. Everyone is, alas, agreed that British broadcasts in French are very poor. In fact, the BBC has lost many listeners in the last weeks, and everyone is listening to Boston and to Switzerland."

Buckmaster replied that the British broadcasts to the French were being overhauled, but in the meantime congratulations were in order. The SOE had made Virginia its first woman field officer. The rank gave her more authority with the Resistance fighters.

In the war-torn months of 1942, Virginia Hall had the monumental job of funding, training, and arming various Resistance groups and freedom fighters, numbering in the thousands of patriots, and bringing them together to fight for a common cause.

She set up many safe houses for those fleeing from the Gestapo. She found places to store weapons. She recruited new agents, supplying them with false names and papers. She organized and further trained Resistance fighters. She managed the return to England of dozens of downed American and British air crews. Amazingly, she was able to recruit into the network officers in Marshal Pétain's government who supplied her with invaluable information.

There were times when Virginia grew impatient with the SOE. In one message to England, she said, "I have learned that nine de Gaulle officers have landed in the past couple weeks. I need to be kept informed of the identity of such men and when they land to avoid any tragic mistakes."

One of these mistakes occurred when Gerry Morel, a British agent, was dropped by plane to assist Virginia in training French fighters in sabotage. The planes used were British Lysanders, known as the Moon Squadron because they flew just before and after the full moon when light was clear. Morel's Lysander was off target, however, and the hapless agent landed in a vineyard a considerable distance from Lyons. He wandered for weeks before reaching a safe house. Only six weeks into operations, he was betrayed by one of his contacts and arrested. He became ill and needed surgery. Dr. Rousset made sure that, following surgery, the agent was trans-ferred to his clinic for round-the-clock care that could not be provided in the hospital.

The Germans approved of this arrangement for they wanted him well enough and awake enough to be questioned. After questioning, his health would be of no concern for he would be shot.

On the same day, Sister Agnes brought one of the sisters from the convent to Dr. Rousset's clinic. Word soon spread that the nun had died. It was a small but sober funeral procession that moved slowly through the streets of Lyons. A horse-drawn hearse led the way up the hill to the convent. The body, of course, was Agent Morel who, after a short recovery period, was provided with safe passage back to England. Once again, Virginia was left to manage the network alone.

As more British agents entered France, Virginia directed them to areas where sabotage could be effectively carried out: power stations, munitions factories, and railroads. After each hit, she prepared a report to be radioed back to London. One of her most efficient radio operators was Denis Rake.

On a late afternoon in June 1942, Virginia found a note slipped under her door. Denis was in danger. His cover had been blown, and he was high on the Gestapo's wanted list. She quickly contacted the Catins to deliver a message to Denis, and made arrangements to meet him at Dr. Rousset's clinic.

"Here are papers and tickets that should get you to London," she told him. "Memorize the address of Madame Long. She will provide a safe house near Paris and pass you on to the Underground who will see you safely out of France."

"What about my wireless?" Denis asked.

"It will be sent first to Paris, then on to London," Virginia assured him.

Instead of following instructions to take the escape route Virginia laid out, Denis went to Paris to look for his wireless set. He was arrested, but escaped while being transported with other prisoners to Dijon.

An aggravated Virginia set up a second escape route, but again the foolish radio operator went to Paris and was arrested getting off the train in the Paris station. In the company of a group of prisoners being herded into transport trucks bound for Germany, Denis managed to escape a second time, but was quickly recaptured. This time, Virginia could do nothing to help.

By late summer 1942, Virginia had increased her trips to the countryside to find sheltered fields for airdrops. She supplied nine trusted agents with money and supplies, and made every attempt to coordinate the activities of a vast network of Resistance groups. Because of her extensive contacts, it was amazing she was not yet on the Gestapo's wanted list; but that was soon to change.

In August, Virginia received word from Dr. Rousset that she might want to meet with a new agent. His name was Abbé Robert Alesh. He knew the passwords and Dr. Rousset had no reason to doubt the man. The abbé was well known for his anti-Nazi sermons and his praise of Charles de Gaulle.

Virginia felt uneasy about such a meeting. "I'll come to the clinic to pay a bill while he is there. Do not reveal my identity to him. I'll listen in another room while you question him."

"My contact in Paris has been arrested," the abbé told Dr. Rousset. "To continue my work, I will need money and new contacts."

Watching through a crack in the door, Virginia saw a small man with a thin, hawklike face and sly, restless eyes. He spoke French with a German accent.

As soon as they were alone, Virginia spoke to the doctor. "Something about that man spells German agent to me," she warned. "Don't give him any information until I have contacted London."

"FOOLS!" she yelled when she received London's reply. She was told the abbé was a reliable agent. Not only was she to supply him with money, she was to forward his intelligence data to London.

She refused to do both.

In November, a flood of German troops poured into

Vichy. Only a month earlier, twelve agents were caught and put in prison. In an attempt to find out who they were, Virginia sent a package to the prison for them; but it was returned, saying there were no such prisoners. She received an unsigned telegram. It urged her to come immediately to the hospital where another agent was very ill. She knew the agent was not in the hospital. It was a trap.

Another letter, left in the consulate letterbox, asked Virginia for five thousand francs to arrange the escape of Justin, a Most Wanted agent who had been captured. She ignored the letter. The next day, Justin arrived with two other men. Virginia sent them to a safe house. It was clear there was a traitor in the Resistance.

Virginia's suspicions grew. The traitor had to be Abbé Alesh. For months, she refused to meet with him. London was wrong. She was sure he was a Gestapo agent.

Unfortunately, she was right! Before the end of November 1942, Virginia's network collapsed. Dr. Rousset was the first to be arrested.

Shortly after the arrest, a sympathetic abbé arrived at the doctor's home and spoke to his assistant, who knew nothing of the doctor's Resistance activities. The abbé asked where he might find the American woman. The assistant did not know, but he did know some of the mutual friends of the doctor and the woman. He innocently gave the abbé the names of other Resistance members. Within a few days, Germaine Guérin was arrested, as were the Joulians. The abbé had done his work well. Now he had only to find the whereabouts of the American woman.

Early one evening, Madame Andrée Michel, another of Virginia's trusted couriers, answered the door of her flat to find Abbé Alesh. He told her, "Odille and her mother have been arrested. She was my only contact with the Resistance. I need to get in touch with the American woman."

Fortunately, Madame Michel shared Virginia's suspicions of the abbé. "Meet me at the Cafe Roulett tomorrow night at nine," she told him. It would give her time to warn Virginia.

Later that same evening, she slipped a note under Virginia's door. It read: This notice has been posted all over France. You must leave at once.

The woman who limps is one of the most dangerous Allied agents in France. We must destroy her.
—The Gestapo, November 1942

Virginia paced the floor of her small flat. She was now at the top of the Gestapo's Most Wanted list. What should she do? There was much work unfinished. More airdrop sites were needed along with more safe houses for downed pilots, but these were harder and harder to find since the German High Command had printed a notice in the paper warning that "any person directly or indirectly helping the crew of enemy aircraft landed by parachute or forced landing or hiding or helping them in any way will be shot immediately."

Yes, there was much work to be done, but Virginia knew nothing could be done if she were standing in front of a firing squad. She had no choice. She must leave, *but,* she thought, *only for a short time.* The only escape route led across the Pyrenees Mountains into Spain. November, she knew, was not a good month for mountain climbing.

Waiting until dark, Virginia gathered a few lumps of coal and newspaper and shoved them into her small stove. She lit the paper, but the coal was slow in catching fire. She blew on it and sneezed as the black smoke tickled her nose. Slowly the flames grew, licking the sides of the grate. Virginia searched through drawers and boxes and other hiding places for ration books, identity papers, and other forged papers. All went into the flames.

She dressed quickly, pulling on a woolen skirt and heavy sweater. She went through the flat one more time to be sure she had missed nothing that might be useful to the enemy. She packed her small, well-worn suitcase with a few pieces of clothing and a little food. Another small bag contained money for the Resistance forces. She grabbed her worn woolen coat and scarf and left the apartment, not bothering to lock the door. Her only stop would be at the home of Nicola, who handled finances for the group.

The city streets were deserted. The last lights of Lyons had long vanished. A sharp wind teased about her nose and mouth, urging her to walk faster. A thin drizzle turned into an icy rain as she hurried along an avenue bordered with leafless trees. She buried her face in her coat. She was shivering, partly from the cold and partly from the job she must finish before she could leave. Would Nicola answer her unexpected knock, or would she sense danger and leave through a back entrance?

A heavy clattering of boots forced Virginia into the shadows. Two gendarmes passed without seeing her. She gave a small sigh of relief. Nicola's flat was two doors down. But wait! Why was there a light in the window this late at night? Virginia could not waste the time to determine if there was trouble. She had to arrive at the train station before the last train left at 11:00 that night.

Fortunately, her knock was answered by her trusted friend. Without a word she shoved the bag of money into Nicola's hands and disappeared into the night.

As Virginia made her way to the railway station, she thought about these ordinary people who showed such courage in fighting the enemy. Not just in France, but people all over Europe who feared and hated Hitler's armies for invading their countries and enslaving their people. Most evil of all was Hitler's determination to imprison millions of an entire group of people, the Jewish people, and erase them from the face of the earth. The madman and his armies had to be stopped!

The railroad station was crowded, noisy, and dirty. The stained floor was spotted with spilled drinks dried in crazy patterns. Crumpled newspapers and wrappers were scattered everywhere. The smell of unwashed bodies permeated the air. Anxious travelers crowded together three deep on the platform, waiting for the train to Perpignan.

Virginia bought her ticket without incident and breathed a sigh of relief. No one paid attention to the plain-looking woman in the heavy coat, dragging a battered suitcase. The train was late as usual. The crowd grew impatient. Hearing a mournful whistle in the distance, the crowd pushed and shoved, each person trying to find a place in the front of the platform.

The huge black engine, spewing smoke and fiery sparks, pulled into the station in a great puff of steam. Slipping between two burly Frenchmen, Virginia boarded the train and sank gratefully into a seat. As tired as she was, sleep would not come. She sat, eyes wide open, the quietness of the car broken only by the clickety-clack of the wheels hitting the rails.

It was a bleary-eyed Virginia who stepped off the train in the early afternoon. Perpignan was a town of narrow streets and tightly packed houses at the foot of mountains that cast deep shadows from the hazy sun.

Stiff from sitting up all night, Virginia walked a bit, then found a small cafe on the square. She slid quietly into a seat by a corner window. The tattered menu had many items crossed off. The war had made food scarce everywhere. A fat man at the next table had finished a huge plate of boiled potatoes. He asked for another. Virginia ordered a bowl of soup. It was cold, but she did not want to call attention to herself by sending it back. She sat for a long time, sipping the sour-tasting soup. She listened without interest to the murmur of voices around her. Her eyes never left the main square of the town.

At last she saw the person she was looking for. Gilbert, another agent, was known to be in the square between 2:00 and 3:00 every day. No one knew where he lived. It was the only way to contact him. Today he was late. It was after three. Virginia did not know Gilbert, but instructions told her to watch for a man wearing a shabby blue jacket with a red scarf around his neck.

Virginia paid her bill, way too much for the thin, sour soup, and left the cafe. She did not approach Gilbert directly but dropped a blue kerchief, gazing at him as she picked it up. It was the signal of one agent to another. He motioned her to follow him. Tucking his flat cap under his arm, Gilbert led Virginia up and down cobbled streets. Once, she stumbled on the uneven cobbles, but Gilbert did not slow his pace. The trip through the back alleys and streets of Perpignan seemed endless. At last they reached a tumbledown gate and a stone path leading to a low house among the trees. Heavy vines climbed past darkened windows.

"In here." Gilbert motioned Virginia through the thick wooden door. She sat in an old horsehair chair that had seen better days. A small fire flickered behind a black iron grate. A large upturned box covered with a faded orange cloth served as a table. Gilbert filled a brown teapot with water from a stone sink and reached for cups from a makeshift shelf. The same shelf held his boot polishing rags and shaving equipment.

Gilbert put water to boil for tea. "The escape route over the mountains must be taken on foot," he explained.

"There is no other way. There is a Spanish guide who will take you for a fee. Do you have money?"

Virginia nodded yes.

Gilbert looked at this determined woman with the wooden leg. He shook his head. "The slopes on the French side of the Pyrenees are very steep. Even if you manage to stay below the heavy snow line, there will be deep snow to get through. Once you cross to the Spanish side, there is little vegetation for cover or shelter. This is no time of year to cross mountains on foot," he warned.

She had no choice. It was the mountains or the Gestapo. Gilbert handed Virginia a cup of steaming tea and left her alone. She blew hard on her tea to cool it while she waited. He was gone more than an hour. Virginia was considering other ways to make her escape when he returned with three other men. One, Leon Guttman, was an Australian. Another, Jean Albert, was part English and part French. The third was a Belgian captain. They also wanted to make the trip but had no money. The Spanish guide refused to take them without being paid.

Virginia laughed and said, "Misery loves company." She would pay 55,000 francs for all of them when they met the guide in the small town of Lavelanet, twenty-eight miles from the border. "Let's go!"

There was no talking on the two-hour drive to Lavelanet. The guide, Juan, was waiting with rucksacks and boots. Virginia paid half his fee. Their climb, through the silver firs of the lower slopes, began at midnight. The journey would take them to Villefranche, over the Col de Tivoli, then down from Camprodon to the railroad station at San Juan de las Abasedas. They moved in complete silence. Border guards, some French and some German, were everywhere. It was bitter cold, as Virginia expected it to be. With the passing hours, the granite and limestone slopes got steeper and steeper, the snow heavier. Luminous snow peaks rose before them to a height of 11,000 feet.

Hour after hour, the party moved steadily with no talking and little rest. Cold winds hit their faces like snapping rubber bands. The drifting snow called on all of Virginia's strength to lift and move her wooden leg. They could not take time to make a fire. They ate cold biscuits on the move. Despite the fiery pain that shot up her thigh, Virginia kept pace, moving as quickly as any of the men. They traveled in the freezing, aching wilderness for seven hours.

Just before dawn, they reached a small cabin. It was cold, but it was shelter and contained six cots with tattered wool blankets. The stump on Virginia's leg was raw and blistered. She covered it with a dry sock, biting her lip with the pain. Juan made a small fire, and the travelers slept there for several hours before resuming their grueling journey. The snow cover was heavy, more than two feet. The biting wind increased from twenty to forty miles per hour. The travelers pressed on in silence over the rough mountain path enveloped in an icy fog. They reached a level of 8,000 feet before they began their descent. At that level, they found themselves gasping for air. They breathed easier as they started downward.

Later that day, the guide pointed to lights just beyond a thick band of trees. Virginia let out a HOOT! "A village in the middle of nowhere," she said, shaking her head with wonder, as Juan led them to a sprawling cabin at the edge of the village.

The white pine door swung open, and they were greeted with the smell of wax and coffee and burning wood, and by a very tall man with a thick yellow beard and long fair hair that hung over his ears. Virginia sank gratefully into a basket chair by the stone fireplace, sipping hot coffee and looking out with wonder at the white world they had conquered. The wind had dropped. The sky was clear. There was warmth from the fire but, best of all, the man had a radio. Virginia sent a coded message to the SOE. As part of her message she added, "Cuthbert is giving me trouble, but I can cope."

Relieved to hear from Virginia, London sent an immediate reply, telling her, "If Cuthbert is giving you trouble, have him eliminated." It was obvious the operator had no idea Cuthbert was Virginia's name for her wooden leg.

The worst of the trip was over. After a night's rest, the travelers began the last stage of their journey. The sun had not yet risen when Juan left them weary but safe at the Spanish border. Light snowflakes were falling when they reached the station at San Juan de las Abasedas and entered one at a time. While they pretended not to know each other, they could not resist grins of relief. They sat apart on separate rusty iron benches. The train to Barcelona would arrive in a little less than an hour. Barcelona would be a stopping point before they finally boarded a ship for England.

A dark shadow loomed across the platform. A Spanish policeman thought four tired, ragged-looking travelers looked suspicious. "Your papers," he demanded.

Virginia looked up from polished boots and brass button uniform into cold blue eyes. It was an implacable face of authority. As if summoned by telepathy, three more police arrived.

No one had papers. Virginia, along with the three men, was arrested and taken to the infamous Figueres prison, a fortress from where escape was impossible.

CHAPTER 11

From Prison to Parties

Virginia's cell was filthy, smelly, and overrun with rats and cockroaches. Walls were a dirty gray plaster with deep cracks in the ceiling, and a floor of stone slabs glistened with damp. She used the wall to mark off with a rusty spoon the passing days. There was no bed, only a thin blanket to wrap around herself to fight the chill from the cold floor. Faint light came from one smoking, swaying lantern outside the cell. One morning, bored with nothing to do, she counted 116 cockroaches on one wall. At night, she covered her face with a scarf to keep the bugs from crawling into her mouth and eyes. Still, it was better than a Gestapo prison or a firing squad.

For once, Virginia did not have a plan. The prisoners were heavily guarded. There was no way to contact the SOE, nor anyone on the outside.

Two weeks passed. Fluent in Spanish, Virginia struck up a conversation with a woman in the next cell. There was little the woman didn't know about Figueres. She had been there six months and was due for release soon. She promised Virginia that, once she was released, she would let the American consul know of her plight. The following day, the woman was gone.

Would she keep her promise? Virginia wondered. There was no way to tell.

Days went by. Virginia paced her prison cell. Surely, the woman had told someone about the American prisoner in Figueres. Or had she?

Six weeks after her arrest, a filthy and much thinner Virginia was released. Her cell door opened and there stood a representative from the American embassy. He had talked to the Spanish authorities. He assured them Virginia was "an American citizen, a newspaper woman, who was no threat to anyone."

The Spaniards believed him. Virginia walked out of jail a free woman and traveled to Lisbon where she boarded a ship for England.

Upon her return to London, she ended a memo to Buckmaster by saying, "I want to go back to France as soon as possible. If you approve, I can change my appearance a bit. There are two men who came out with me I would like to take back. One is Australian and the other French-English. Both will be valuable agents. Can you speed up our return?"

Virginia was disappointed once again. Her request was denied.

Virginia's difficult and dangerous trip across the

Pyrenees Mountains was followed by five months of doing very little in London. In May 1943, she opened a memo from Buckmaster. As she read the contents, she shook her head in disgust at the new assignment. She was to spend the next several months in Spain as an undercover agent for the SOE. Her cover was as a foreign correspondent for the *Chicago Times*.

Buckmaster warned Virginia, "Do nothing for the first few months. Convince everyone you are a legitimate reporter and there only for the purpose of gathering news. At the same time, keep your eyes and ears open and report any suspicious behavior to us."

Virginia quickly discovered that Madrid was a city of spies. German, American, British, and Japanese agents made Madrid their temporary home. Even some officials in the British embassy felt that spying in a neutral country (Spain) was wrong and gave no help to British agents. It was wisest to trust no one.

Going to parties and listening to gossip was the last thing Virginia wanted to do. She was worried about her friends in France. What had happened to Nicola and Monsieur Labourier? She was sure Abbé Alesh had reported them by now. Virginia had to know their fate, but there was no way she could find out. Even in Spain, if she asked questions about members of the French Resistance, she would be suspect.

For a woman who had risked her life daily as an agent in France, who had barely escaped the Gestapo, and who had made the grueling trip across the mountains, she considered this assignment a waste.

On October 1, Virginia wrote to Buckmaster, "I've given this a good four months' try and have come to the conclusion that it really is a waste of time and money. Anyhow, I always did want to go back to France, and now I have had the luck to find two of my own boys here (two agents Virginia worked with in France who had escaped over the mountains as she had) and will send them on to you. They want me to go back with them because we worked together before and our teamwork is good. I suggest I go back as their radio (operator) or else aider and abettor as before. I can learn the radio quickly enough, in spite of skeptics in some quarters. When I came out here (to Spain) I thought I would be able to help F-Section people, but I don't and can't. I am not doing a job. I am simply living pleasantly and wasting time. It isn't worthwhile, and all, my neck is my own, and I'm willing to get a crick in it because there is a war on, I do think...Well, anyhow, I put it up to you. I think I can do a job for you along with my two boys. They think I can, too, and I trust you will let us try, because we are all three very much in earnest about this bloody war."

The reply from Buckmaster was quick in coming.

Virginia read the letter twice. It was not what she wanted to hear.

> Dearest Doodles (Virginia),
> What a wonder you are! I know you
> could learn radio in no time. I know the
> boys would love to have you in the field.
> I know all about the things you could do,
> and it is only because I honestly believe
> that the Gestapo would also know it in
> about a fortnight that I say NO, dearest
> Doodles, NO. You are really too well
> known in the country and it would be
> wishful thinking to believe that you could
> escape detection for more than a few
> days. You do realize, don't you, that what
> was previously a picnic, comparatively
> speaking, is now the real war and that
> the Gestapo are pulling in everything
> they can? You will object, I know, that
> it is your own neck. I agree. But we all
> know it is not only your own neck. It is
> the necks of all with whom you come
> into contact because the Boche is good at
> patiently following trails and sooner or
> later, he will unravel the whole skein if he

has a chance. We do not want to give him even half a chance by sending in anyone as remarkable as yourself at the moment. If you do not feel you are pulling your weight where you are, why not come back to London and join us as a briefing officer for the boys? Your duties would be:

(a) Meet them when they come back from the field, to hear what they have to say, to analyze it, and to see they get their questions answered.

(b) See that they are properly looked after from the point of view of material things, i.e., clothes, equipment, etc.

(c) Brief the new boys with the fruits you have yourself learned and what you have picked up from the latest arrivals.

This, I know, sounds like a sit-down job of the same type you are doing now, but it has this possible, repeat possible, advantage. If and when officers from here go into the field round about D-Day, you will be in the right place to start from. I obviously can make no promises as to this at the moment, but it is a possibility.

Signed: M.B. (Maurice Buckmaster)

As unhappy as she was with Buckmaster's reply, Virginia returned to London. Anything was better than doing nothing in Spain. Fortunately, Virginia did have one of her requests granted. She made friends with the sergeant who repaired damaged radios. His workshop was a tangled mess of wires and bolts and machine parts. "Teach me to operate and repair a radio," she said, "and I'll clean up your mess."

After that, she met with returning agents during the day, but every night she put things right in the radio room while she trained to qualify as a radio operator. In her job as a briefing officer, Virginia heard other agents talking about a new American spy organization, the OSS, that was joining forces with the SOE.

"At last!" Virginia smiled. "Whether they know it or not, I'm finally serving my own country. Maybe ambassadors can't have one leg, but it's a good thing there is no such rule for female spies."

She was right! Early in 1944, General Bill Donovan of the OSS arrived in London to meet with Buckmaster. He took one look at Virginia's record and the two agreed it was time to give her a new assignment.

"You are to return to France," Buckmaster told her. "You will collect as much information about German troop movements as you can. D-Day, when France will be invaded by American and British troops, is in the planning stages. Trained Resistance fighters could be invaluable in its success. One of your tasks is to train and equip these fighters. In addition, you will continue to find ideal fields for parachute drops and locate more safe houses in and near Paris." He then grinned. "Your newly acquired radio skills will allow you instant communication with us."

Virginia was surprised Buckmaster knew about her radio training.

It was a huge assignment and a highly dangerous one. "When do I leave?" she asked.

Returning to her apartment to pack, Virginia let out a yell, "Cuthbert, we're going back to France!"

One of the first things she planned to do was locate friends who had been so loyal and who had not been arrested: Madame Landry, who obtained much-needed fake papers; and Marquis d'Aragon, who hid downed French and American flyers in his chateau.

DURING THIS TIME IN THE WORLD

1944 The Beginning of the End

On June 1, 1944, the first line of a poem by Paul Verlaine was broadcast by the BBC to French Resistance fighters, indicating the invasion of France by the Allies was near. The night of June 5, the second line of the Verlaine poem was broadcast. The invasion was on!

On D-Day (June 6), also known as Operation Overlord, 155,000 Allied troops landed on the beaches of Normandy, in France. The invasion included Allied land forces that came from Great Britain, the United States, Canada, and the Free French. Polish forces also participated, along with fighting men from Belgium, Czechoslovakia, Greece, and the Netherlands.

To support the invasion, Jedburgh teams parachuted into France and joined the French Resistance against the German occupiers. There were ninety-three three-man teams, each with two officers and a radio operator. Trained as commandos, they were truly soldiers of fortune. After landing, the teams coordinated airdrops of arms and supplies, guided the partisans on hit-and-run attacks and sabotage, and did their best to assist the advancing Allied armies.

In early August, the Allies captured Florence, Italy; and, on August 25, the Allies liberated Paris after four years of occupation by the Germans. American troops, numbering 1.2 million and commanded by General Omar Bradley, had the German army in retreat.

CHAPTER 12

Back to France

A British gunboat, hidden in a thickening fog, approached the rocky and wind-whipped Brittany Coast. Moving in as closely as possible, motors were shut down. A dinghy was lowered, and silent oars dipped through murky waters. In the distance, forbidding mountains cast deep shadows against a gray and misty sky. The dinghy held two passengers who, at first glance, appeared to be an old man and an old woman, their peasant clothing sewn exactly as if it had been made in France rather than in England. From eyeglasses to shoes, every item worn by either person was as perfect as if it were made in the local area. Virginia Hall was returning to France! The date was March 14, 1944.

Operating under the code name of Diane Heckler, Virginia was anxious to begin her second tour of duty as a spy in France. To avoid capture, Virginia had created a new disguise. She needed to move about freely and avoid suspicion. With her milking skills gained from her days at Box Horn Farm, she turned herself into an old farm woman. She dyed her soft brown hair a dirty gray. She wore heavy woolen clothes to look fatter. She taught herself to swing her wooden leg as she walked so she did not limp.

Tucking her long skirts around her waist, she stepped out of the dinghy, ignoring the icy water that crept over the edge of her worn black leather boots. In one hand was a battered suitcase containing the newest in radio transmitters that would allow her to talk with planes circling overhead. Without stopping, she waded through the shallows and reached the rocky shore, climbing rapidly like a mountain goat, her long wool skirt unfurling behind her like a sail caught in the wind.

"Wait!" a voice called out. With her was another American agent, code name, Aramis. This time, Virginia would not be working alone.

But something was wrong. Aramis was far down the path, his somewhat chubby body bent over, clutching his left knee. Caught by a devious root, he missed a step and fell, twisting his knee in the process. Their destination, the town of Morlaix, was five miles away. It was obvious Aramis could not make the journey that night.

Virginia ripped off part of her underskirt. "Bind the knee tight with this," she said, picking up a sturdy piece of wood and handing it to the man. "Use this as a crutch."

The two made their way slowly up the steep, wet path and across a dark and stubby field. In the distance was the sprawling shape of a farmhouse with windows dimly lit.

"We'll have to chance it," Virginia said when they reached the weather-beaten house. She set down her suitcase, reached up, and knocked on the heavy wooden door. A jolly little woman, her hair dark and tightly braided, opened the door and showed no surprise at the travelers. Since the fall of Paris, two million people had taken to the roads out of the city, walking or riding bikes. There was no money for fuel. One more elderly couple begging food at her door was not unusual.

"Pardon, Madame," Virginia said. "We are on our way to visit our daughter in Morlaix, but my husband has injured his leg. Could we perhaps sleep in your barn tonight and continue our journey in the morning?"

"But, of course," the woman answered. She led them to a barn where they could spend the rest of the night. Virginia signaled Aramis to say nothing. He ignored her signal and chatted away to the woman, even telling her his name. Virginia was astounded. The first rule of a foreign agent was to say absolutely nothing, trust no one. She vowed to ditch Aramis as soon as possible.

Virginia's assignment was to join the Resistance in the Haute-Loire region of central France. She would set up sabotage and guerrilla groups and supply them with money, arms, and rations. Aramis had a different assignment with headquarters in Paris.

The next morning, Virginia and Aramis left the farm and made their way to the train station in Morlaix. German troops were everywhere, but no one paid attention to the limping man and the stooped gray-haired old woman. They left the train just outside Paris. The streets were nearly deserted. The few passersby stared at the sidewalks, never lifting their eyes to others.

They soon reached the home of Madame Long, the woman who had befriended Virginia four years earlier. Plump and wrinkled, Madame Long was not anyone's image of a Resistance fighter. Her croissants melted on the tongue, and her hearty laugh could be heard three houses away.

"Welcome, welcome, old friend," she hugged Virginia. "Now who is this? A pretty girl who looks like an old woman. And who is your companion?"

"Peter Harratt, at your service, madame." Madame Long was as shocked as Virginia. Brash and smiling and way too amiable, this agent appeared to have no sense at all. He should know that anyone who smiles all the time needs watching, and his willingness to engage a stranger in conversation was unthinkable.

"This man is not welcome here," she told Virginia. "Get rid of him." By that same evening, Virginia found Aramis a safe place to stay, but she warned trusted friends not to tell him anything. He was to meet his contact the next day in Paris.

There was no way Virginia would place Madame Long in danger. She was a trusted friend who never refused a request. She provided a safe house for those escaping from the Gestapo, collected clothing for escapees, delivered messages, and was soon to help in another way, by traveling with Virginia on many vital missions. It was unsafe for Virginia to travel alone because her slight American accent would be questioned. Madame Long would do all the talking whenever the two traveled together.

The following day, Virginia left Madame Long and made a two-hour journey by train to the small village of Creuse.

As an old farm woman, she needed cows to milk. Virginia knew that people in the country were more likely to help the Resistance than city dwellers. She remembered a report she had sent to the SOE two years earlier. She had informed Buckmaster that the country folk were turning more and more against the government and toward the English. The farmers were angry at having to get their seed from the authorities and being forced to hand over fifty to ninety-nine percent of the harvest. Many farmers stopped planting. What was the use if they had to give it all to the Germans?

Virginia found a farmer who was happy to hire her as a milkmaid. During the day, she delivered milk, gathering information on her rounds. Each evening she brought the cows in from pasture. She hid her radio in the farmer's barn.

Virginia detailed her life in Creuse in this report to Buckmaster:

> Aramis accompanied me to Creuse in spite of a very painful knee, which he sprained during our landing on the coast. In Creuse, I contacted farmer Eugene Lopinat, who found a little house for me with one room, no water or electricity, located by the side of the road at the other end of the village from his farmhouse. He arranged for me to eat and work at his own house. Here I cooked for the farmer, his old mother, and the hired hand, over an open fire as there was no stove in the house. I took his cows to pasture and, in the process, found several good fields for parachute drops. Aramis returned to Paris to start his own work and to arrange a courier service to come to me at Maidou.

Sometimes Virginia herded goats instead of cows. The German patrol cars roared by, paying little attention to the old woman and her goats. They laughed when she pretended to choke from the dusty road and truck fumes. They did not know that her sharp eyes were watching for fields that would make excellent parachute drops. After radioing the information to London, she waited for a message that gave her the time and place of the next drop.

"Stay out of sight," she said to the men who accompanied her on a typical night when a drop was scheduled. The men went off separately and silently to a field surrounded by a dark woods. There they waited, hidden by the trees, until they heard the faint roar of Lysanders overhead. Every rustle, every slapping branch or snapping twig could mean danger.

As soon as they heard the dull purring of the Lysander, Virginia and three of the men formed a diamond shape and turned on their flashlights. This was the drop area that could be seen from the plane. On this night they were lucky. A parachute with a large bundle attached almost dropped into their hands. They turned off their lights and unclipped the parachute. While two of the Resistance fighters buried the chute, the others loaded the weapons, ammunition, and other supplies into a donkey cart. The group disappeared as quietly as it had gathered, with two of the men leading the donkey cart to a hiding place known only to a few.

Nights when no drops were scheduled, Virginia radioed reports of troop movements. The Germans were getting better and better at locating radio signals. They had planes with radio direction finders. When a radio location was found, it was bombed. Virginia could not keep her radio in the farmer's barn. She had to move it often. She knew every time she sent a message she could be caught. She did not stop. In one month, she sent thirty-seven messages.

Early one morning, while Virginia was at her milking chores, she looked up in dismay to see Aramis framed by the barn door.

"Ho, Heckler," he called out, as if code names were a joke. "I come bearing messages." Life in Paris appeared to have been good to him. He had gained weight; his round body was even rounder. His old-man disguise was gone and he sported straw-colored hair. His suit was of light wool, stylishly cut, his shirt had a high white collar, and his pointed boots shone like black glass. Virginia's first thought was he had probably been followed.

"You fool," Virginia spit. "Your mouth is running off as usual. You are never to come here again. If messages are necessary, send them by the courier network."

"Whatever you say." Aramis looked relieved. "Trips

away from Paris are very tiring," he whined. "It takes me three days to recover from each trip." The truth was, he disliked the dirty, smelly trains, and much preferred his comfortable Paris apartment. At the same time, he was somewhat resentful. He could not understand why he, as an American agent, could not be trusted to deliver important messages.

Virginia's report to the SOE concerning Aramis read: "I found a few good fields for receptions, and farmers and farm hands eager to help. Aramis came twice but with nothing to report except having found...an old family friend, whose flat he might use as a safe house. He did not seem to understand using couriers, or the advisability of so doing, and fiercely resented any suggestions. Aramis claims the trips are very tiring. In spite of his robust appearance, he says he is not very strong, cannot carry parcels or packages of any weight, because he has no strength in his arms, and he says he is ill for a few days after each trip."

Buckmaster had sent Virginia to France trusting in her good judgment, great courage, and cool head to pull the Resistance fighters together and be ready to support the Allied troops landing on D-Day. Aramis was putting them all in danger with his unnecessary visits. The Gestapo noose was tightening. French citizens were being gunned down over the slightest infraction of German law.

Visits by Aramis had to be stopped before he exposed the whole network.

OSS agent Peter Harratt, code name Aramis,
drew this picture of Virginia,
code name Diane Heckler, in 1944.
National Archives, Records of the Office of Strategic Services

CHAPTER 13

Cat and Mouse

Virginia knew it was time to move, and this time her location would be kept secret from Aramis. Staying in one place too long was dangerous.

One of the greatest difficulties in Virginia's work was finding safe houses. Pierre, a trusted courier, no sooner told Virginia he had found three safe houses in Tours, than the first house was raided, the radio operator was arrested, and the whole area was teeming with Gestapo. Virginia left the Lopinat farm at night and set off for Cosno with another good and trusted friend, Madame Rabut. Madame Rabut was a short, slightly plump woman with scanty white hair. She spoke in a loud voice as if hard of hearing. Virginia wore her usual layers of heavy clothing, her dirty gray hair visible under a worn woolen scarf. As expected, no one bothered two old chattering women.

In Cosno, she found shelter in the attic of another friend, Madame Vessereau, a person of importance in the village, for she was the wife of the local police chief. Madame was a social butterfly with large brown eyes and a laughing mouth. Everyone adored her and admired her husband who made no attempt to enforce the new laws imposed by the Germans. The Gestapo never discovered that radio messages to the Americans and the British were sent from the police chief's home.

Despite the dangers of frequent broadcasting, Virginia kept London well informed. In one message she told Buckmaster, "It is sometimes difficult to decide where money for goods will do the most good. Nicholas, who received a large quantity of explosives, gave them to other organizations, which used the stuff to carry out irritating acts with no real value. I've seen material badly stored in damp places and ruined, with even the plastic showing signs of mold. One Resistance group foolishly blew up the rails in front of a train carrying Pétain, not to hurt him but only to frighten him. There are too many groups and each seems to want to outdo the other."

Attempting to unify the groups into an effective fighting force was a monumental task. In Virginia's area, five groups were dominant, each led by a man more concerned with his own importance than in taking orders from London through Virginia. At the same time, more and more Resistance groups were forming, each appealing to Virginia for arms and munitions. Battalions of Frenchmen waiting in the hills were growing restless and were eager to attack. However, before they were given money and arms, Virginia insisted they must take their orders from the SOE as to targets to be hit. One thorn in her side was an officious colonel. He wanted to take all the arms and do as he pleased with them.

"Madame," the colonel told Virginia, "the Resistance fighters are strong, brave, and courageous men. Many have the rank of captain or higher. You have no rank at all. They refuse to take orders from a woman. Therefore, we will determine our own targets and have no intention of taking orders from the British."

Virginia slapped the tabletop in an impatient air of disgust. "These men are like little boys wanting to play war regardless of the consequences," she said. "Very well, those who refuse to take orders from London through me can then find another source of money and arms."

The fighters soon discovered there was no other source of money and arms. After that, Virginia's instructions were followed with minor grumbling, and the flow of arms continued. Bren guns, submachine guns, rifles, plastic explosives, and ammunition were dropped from the skies by parachute or delivered by night landings of RAF Lysanders that skirted the edges of meadows, stirring up the dust of pollen and hay.

In addition to those who bore arms, the Resistance had jobs for everyone who wanted to fight the Germans:

factory owners, couriers, volunteers for safe houses, spotters, field locaters, escorts for escaped prisoners and downed flyers; the list was endless. Virginia was expected to recruit them all.

There were times when she turned down offers of help particularly when the desire to defeat the Germans overcame common sense. Sophie was this kind of a problem. Her hatred of the Nazis was such that she was willing to take on any assignment. However, she was too excitable, dramatic, emotional, and noticeable to be of much use. One assignment she asked Virginia for was to shake the gates of the local jail until all the French prisoners were released. Virginia said, "NO!"

In late April, Virginia had to move again. She returned to her attic room, after a fruitless night of watching for an airdrop, to find Madame Vessereau in tears.

"Oh, my son, my son," she moaned. "Fernand has been arrested as a spy!"

"Arrested? Why?" Virginia asked.

Madame wrung her hands. "As a young captain, he was often in and out of German headquarters in Paris. He saw the German plan for the defense of Paris on the table of his colonel. He could not resist. He copied the plan and was caught with the copies."

Virginia shook her head. She knew there was nothing she could do to help and that, under pressure from the Gestapo, Fernand would reveal Virginia's location.

This time her move was to the Le Puy District and the farm of Madame Leah Lebret, who was to become a dear and trusted friend. Tall and gaunt, thin of face, Madame Lebret had weather-beaten hands that had held the reins of a horse and the handle of a plow. Despite the danger to her family, she had sheltered many downed British flyers at the Lebret farm.

"There is just me and the two children here," Madame told Virginia. "The Germans take the little food I cannot manage to hide. You are welcome to share what we have."

Virginia followed her to a small bedroom with a polished oak floor that reflected the sunlight. It held a brass-knobbed bed, with a handmade quilt, a tall oak wardrobe, and a dressing table. Virginia sat on the bed, sinking down into the soft mattress. She smiled. Having spent much of her time in shacks with no running water or electricity, this was pure luxury. But she could not accept Madame's hospitality. German patrols were everywhere. Hiding Virginia and her radio would put the good woman and her children in constant danger. Virginia had to look elsewhere. She decided on a barn three kilometers away. The distance was not great, so Madame Lebret continued to send Virginia a hot meal every day. In addition, she sent Edmond, her nephew, to operate the generator that supplied power to Virginia's B2 radio. The code phrase *les marguerites fleuriront ce soir* (the daisies will bloom tonight) alerted Virginia to expect a message from London.

Sometimes she had company. On this day, two freedom fighters were concealed in the barn with her when a German patrol car pulled into the yard.

"Quick, out the back," Virginia ordered. "Join the other workers and keep your mouths shut." In her old lady disguise, Virginia shuffled outside. Madame Lebret arrived about the same time with a basket of food. Neither woman spoke.

The Germans made a quick search of the house and barn, finding no one. One soldier turned to Madame Lebret. "Your eyes are always on us," he said. "I believe you have something to hide." Madame did not reply. He whipped the napkin from the top of her basket. "She's hiding bread," he laughed. Helping himself to the warm baked loaf, the soldier slapped his knee and laughed. Madame Lebret gave a sly smile as the patrol car left the farmyard.

One of the men in hiding was Lieutenant Bob. Virginia was soon to discover he was a solid and good man who could be depended upon for any task no matter how large or small. Tall and straight, he had the face of a rascal, intelligent and shrewd with piercing black eyes, unruly hair of the same color, and a deceptively tender smile.

"I've lived in the mountains more than a year, leading groups to do whatever damage we could to the Germans. Unfortunately, we don't have the guns and ammunition to do as much damage as we would like," he told Virginia.

Virginia had a feeling this was the man she needed to help her unite the various Resistance groups into one strong unit.

On June 1, Virginia's wireless tapped out a strange message. It was the first line of a poem by Paul Verlaine. It was code. The invasion of France was near. When the second line of the poem was broadcast, thousands of Allied forces would hit the beaches of France. It would be the beginning of the end for Germany.

The next day, Charlotte Norris in the London office answered an inquiry from Virginia's mother about her daughter's well-being. Her reply read, "From a security point of view, there is little I can tell you about your daughter's work. For this, I am sorry; it may, however, be of some consolation to you that my own husband knows absolutely nothing of my work. But this I can tell you: that your daughter is with the First Experimental Detachment of the United States Army; that she is do- ing an important and time-consuming job which has necessitated a transfer from London, and which will reduce her correspondence to a minimum. We here are in constant touch with your daughter, and are immediately informed of any change in her status. I shall be happy to communicate any news of her to you."

CHAPTER 14

D-Day!

On the night of June 5, 1944, Virginia's wireless burst forth with the second line of the Verlaine poem. The invasion was on! The Allies had assembled an initial landing force of 155,000 troops backed by 5,000 large ships, 4,000 smaller landing craft, and more than 11,000 aircraft. In General Eisenhower's message to the Resistance fighters, he asked for their help; and Virginia, along with thousands of others, was there to give it. By now, she had organized and equipped three battalions of Frenchmen.

"Our first job," she told the men, "is to slow down Germany's Second Panzer Division on its way to the Normandy beaches. The invasion forces need time to establish a stronghold."

London kept Virginia's radio humming: Where was the largest concentration of German troops? Which direction were they heading? Did they have strongholds in any towns or villages? Where was the German general staff?

This last question, Virginia was able to answer quite

by accident on a morning when she and Lieutenant Bob cycled into Le Puy. There they saw heavy trucks and German staff cars unloading at city hall.

Virginia laughed. "We've made life so miserable for them in Lyons, they are moving to Le Puy! They don't know it now, but we will make life just as miserable for them here!" She lost no time in radioing the information to London.

The Central Plateau Region where Virginia operated was rough and rocky, with steep hills. This made traveling very difficult, yet it was essential she keep the Allies informed of both troop movements and the best locations for parachute drops. The weapons and explosives from the drops were put to immediate use.

Night after night, Resistance teams slowed the Germans by destroying bridges and tunnels, cutting phone lines, and derailing freight trains. Virginia ignored orders from the SOE not to lead sabotage groups. On a typical night, Virginia, Lieutenant Bob, and two other Resistance fighters set out in an old truck for their target. On this night, it was an ammunition bunker. It was a dangerous mission. While the men laid crude explosives, Virginia played the part of a foolish old woman. The men had only minutes to light the fuses and get away. When German sentries appeared, Virginia caught their attention.

"Please, help me," she moaned in French. "I have

lost my way. My daughter will be looking for me." As she repeated her plea, the soldiers, who did not speak French, tried communicating with her using hand signals. She pretended not to understand.

Suddenly, there was a tremendous explosion that lit up the night sky. The startled sentries turned their backs on Virginia and quickly rushed to the scene of the explosion.

Virginia raced for the truck. "GO!" she shouted. Lieutenant Bob stepped on the gas, the rickety truck backfiring once as it bounced over the rough roads, to put as much distance as possible between them and the damage they had caused. After they traveled several miles, Lieutenant Bob stopped the truck and the freedom fighters disappeared into the night.

All missions were not as successful, however. Disaster waited when Virginia relayed orders from London to blow up a train that was carrying German arms and ammunition. One freedom fighter had a girlfriend and, unknown to Lieutenant Bob, they had a rocky relationship. The night before the team was to blow up the train, the couple had a big fight, with words loud enough to be heard in the apartment below. The young man slammed out of her apartment, vowing never to see her again.

Acting on intelligence from Virginia regarding the train schedule, the team arrived at the designated spot early the next morning. They placed sticks of dynamite around the rail and waited for the right moment to finish the job. Suddenly, there were Germans everywhere. The quiet mountainside was filled with shouting and the echo of gunshots.

"Scatter!" Lieutenant Bob ordered. "Make for the mountains!"

Several men were shot. Most of the team escaped into the hills. Lieutenant Bob learned several days later that the girlfriend, angry at her boyfriend, had told the Germans of the planned attack on the train.

As Virginia's second-in-command, Lieutenant Bob was fearless, particularly when he put on a Nazi uniform that allowed him to get closer to the action.

Virginia never asked how Lieutenant Bob acquired the uniform that allowed him to spend time at Nazi headquarters in Le Puy. Not being able to speak much German, he mumbled responses to greetings and carried a bottle of wine, appearing to be drunk most of the time. But in this way, he gathered information that was invaluable in planning sabotage attacks.

The damage caused by the Resistance was not without a price. In an appeal to the French people the day after the invasion, Marshal Pétain cautioned, "Do not aggravate our misfortune by acts which risk bringing tragic reprisals upon you. It will be the innocent French population which will suffer the consequences. Do not listen to those who are looking to exploit our distress, who would lead the country to disaster. France will not be saved except by observing the most rigorous discipline. Obey the orders of the government."

These were not just words. Reprisals against the Resistance were swift and cruel. Innocent men and women living in towns and villages where guerrilla warfare took place were put to death. After one such attack by the Resistance to destroy a storage dump, a group of German soldiers entered the village of Oradour-sur-Glane and executed more than 600 men, women, and children, before setting fire to the village.

Despite the reprisals, Virginia, now in charge of 1,500 men, knew she and the Resistance must step up the pace of their activities to give the greatest help to the Allies.

Word came that twelve German lorries were on the Le Puy Road.

"Destroy them," Virginia ordered.

A supply depot was left unguarded for a brief time each evening.

"Send a team to blow it up," Virginia told Lieutenant Bob.

General staff cars were heading for Le Puy.

"Cut them off and surround them," Virginia told the team.

On the morning of August 12, Virginia had a welcome surprise.

"Look what we've caught!" Lieutenant Bob yelled, pointing below. She stood with the lieutenant in a narrow mountain pass, looking through the gray haze that hung over the valley below. During the night, the Resistance had blown the bridges between Chamelix and Pigeyre. Five hundred German soldiers were trapped between the two towns and held captive under the watchful eye of the freedom fighters.

Virginia reported to London:

> The three planeloads of supplies that were
> dropped helped tremendously and enabled
> the men to do a lot of bridge and tunnel
> wrecking (to slow the German retreat) and
> to capture the Germans out of Le Puy by
> sheer bluff, making them surrender, some
> five or six hundred.

Late in the summer, Virginia and her men were stationed at the edge of a wide meadow, waiting for a parachute drop. To her surprise, three men were part of the drop. Virginia had been watching all summer for the Jedburgh teams she was told would arrive. Each team typically had an OSS operative, a British officer, and an enlisted man who handled the radio. Trained as commandos, they were men of both courage and ability.

"Better late than never," Virginia quipped. "I hope one of you is a general."

While most of the Resistance leaders followed the instructions she got from London, there were others who promoted themselves to high ranks so that, despite Virginia's threat to cut off money and ammunition, they felt they did not need to follow orders. One of the colonels, over Virginia's objections, had taken 1,500 poorly trained men into battle against the Germans, an act Virginia considered stupid. There were heavy losses.

After that disaster, the officers in the Jedburgh team pulled rank.

"There will be no operations except those ordered by London. Groups that ignore this order will receive no weapons or ammunition."

Although a few noses were out of joint among higher-ranking French officers, orders from then on generally were carried out without argument.

Even though the Germans had been driven from the area, the first Jedburgh team was quickly followed by two agents, one who was to have a great effect on Virginia's future.

As often happened, the men were dropped a considerable distance from the target site. Virginia considered the

American planes the worst in making drops, saying they were "shoddy at best." The team consisted of two men, Lieutenant Henry Riley and Lieutenant Paul Goillot, an OSS agent from New York.

The men quickly buried their parachutes and dressed as civilians. Their instructions, from the agent named Philomene, were to proceed to Madame Roussier's shop in Le Chambon. Both men were surprised they encountered no German patrols.

"You will find Philomene at Madame Lebret's farm," she said, giving them directions. "Although I don't know what good you can do now. You have arrived too late. The fighting is over. The Germans have fled the district."

In all her years in France, working with the Resistance, Virginia had avoided relationships. While she greatly admired the willingness to fight and organizational ability of Lieutenant Bob, and the sheer courage of Madame Lebret, as well as the dozens of freedom fighters who daily risked their lives, she made every effort not to become so close to an individual that she became emotionally involved. That was why it was so surprising when Virginia met Lieutenant Goillot.

"Paul Goillot at your service, ma'am," he said, finding Virginia in the barn, packing up her wireless.

She looked up into a delicate thin face with soft gray laughing eyes, and a mouth that parted in a charming smile. His chin was covered with a bluish shadow, his body light and slender. His clothing was of thin cheap material. Virginia surprised herself by feeling an instant connection with the smiling lieutenant.

"You are too late for the party," Virginia said, returning the smile. "We are packing up. The Germans have fled."

"If you are packing, you must have a destination," Paul said. "How about some company on your trip?"

"How is it you speak French so fluently?" Virginia asked.

"I am a New Yorker whose family came to the US from France. After a few years they had enough of the Big Apple and went home. I had a good job and there was none waiting for me in France, so I stayed."

"Come along if you wish," Virginia told all the men. "The Germans are on the run in Northern France. They've been chasing me for four years. It's a pleasure to be chasing them for a change."

Virginia and Lieutenant Bob secured a seven-ton truck with a machine gun trained over the cab. Virginia, the two American lieutenants, and a team of Resistance fighters headed north to Alsace, hoping to find a fighting unit they could join. On the road, they caught up with the French Ninth Colonial Infantry Division.

"Where are we needed?" Virginia called out.

An exhausted captain with a week-old beard grinned at Virginia. "No more action here," he replied. "We've cleaned the Boche out. Try the Allied Command Center in Bourg. There could be new assignments there."

Lieutenant Bob made up his mind to join the French Ninth Colonial along with his men. They could be useful in ferreting out hidden pockets of Germans. For a moment, he gazed at this cool-headed, courageous woman he had served with for more than a year. He clasped both her hands in his. "Good luck," he said.

"You, too," Virginia answered. "Let's go," she told Paul Goillot.

Virginia and Paul left for Bourg to offer what help they could in ambush and intelligence. After being shuffled from one officer to another, they came to the conclusion there was no assignment to be had.

"If we can't fight," Paul told Virginia, "let's see what's happening in Paris." The two agreed to give themselves a bit of a holiday, and moved on to liberated Paris and a new assignment.

DURING THIS TIME IN THE WORLD

1945 Victory in Europe

Because of a foolish no-withdrawal order by Hitler, France was liberated by the Allied forces in August 1944, with the capture of 200,000 German troops. February 1945 brought heavy bombardment of Germany by more than 2,000 Allied aircraft.

From February 4–11 the Allied leaders, Roosevelt, Churchill, and Stalin, met in Yalta to discuss postwar plans, which included dividing the country into occupied zones, furnishing the German people with the necessities to survive, controlling all German industry and armament plants, and bringing war criminals to trial.

In March, United States, British, and Canadian forces swept across Germany. On March 19, Hitler issued an order that all gas works, electric plants, waterworks, food and clothing stores should be destroyed, leaving a "desert" for the Allied forces to find. According to Hitler, "If the war is lost, the German nation will perish. There is no need to consider what the people require for continued existence." On April 30, Hitler took his own life. In May 1945, German forces surrendered.

There was great rejoicing among the occupied countries of Europe, yet the task of rebuilding both cities and lives destroyed by the German war machine was just beginning. Allied troops who tore down the gates of concentration camps were devastated to find men, women, and children who were mere skeletons after months of starvation. Families that were torn apart would never be put back together. A War Crimes Commission was established to bring to justice those responsible for crimes against humanity.

CHAPTER 15

The Dream Fulfilled

With the liberation of France by the Allied forces, Virginia was asked to take on a new assignment. Nazi resistance in Austria was fierce, and operatives were needed in that area to train Resistance fighters. She did not hesitate and was especially pleased that Paul Goillot would be traveling with her. It was April 1945, and the two were to travel through Switzerland and on to the Innsbruck area to set up Resistance cells and send back intelligence reports.

Virginia, who had welcomed the assignment, was disappointed when the entire operation was canceled at the last minute. The defeat of the Germans had come much more quickly than expected. Virginia Hall appeared to be out of a job.

After years of living dangerously, Virginia was not ready to return to the States and the peace and quiet of Box Horn Farm. While she and Paul were in France, she was anxious to discover the fate of her friends and to find those traitors who had brought so much grief to many good people.

By summer 1945, Virginia and Paul found great rejoicing in Paris. The hated swastikas were torn from buildings. As rapidly as possible, signs of the German occupation were erased. Street cafes reopened despite the shortage of food. Many had only coffee to serve, made from tree bark, but Parisians enjoyed visiting with each other and calling out to passersby, something that was unheard of during the German occupation.

Collaborators were dealt with harshly. Many were shot. Women collaborators were fortunate if they only had their hair cut off. Others were tarred and feathered.

Not long after D-Day, Pétain and his ministers had fled to Germany. In 1945, leaders of the Vichy government were arrested. Pierre Laval and Joseph Darnand, head of the secret police, were executed. Pétain was sent into exile.

One evening, Paul and Virginia attended a performance by Josephine Baker, the American dancer, who many considered to be a collaborator. Walter Winchell, an American newspaper man, wrote, "While our boys were over there stopping bullets. . . Josephine Baker was living it up, making oodles of dough in Paris, wining and dining the Nazis and Mussolini's bigwig generals."

Despite the criticism, Josephine Baker continued to entertain the Nazis throughout the war, even though her beloved Paris had turned against her. Only the leaders of the French Resistance knew why Josephine danced for the Germans. At the end of each dance, she chatted with high-ranking officers. The Germans talked freely. She learned about troop movements and locations. She obtained an important code book. For four years, despite two severe illnesses, she served France in the Resistance, pretending to be a collaborator. At the end of the war, a grateful France awarded Josephine its highest honors: the Medal of the Resistance, the Légion d'honneur, and the Croix de guerre.

During those first days in Paris, which were supposed to be a time of rest, Virginia wrote SOE and OSS officials about many who had lost everything they had in their efforts to fight the Germans. A letter written to her superiors on June 11, 1945, read:

> Madame Eugenie Catin of Lyon was
> recruited in the early summer of 1942
> as courier for the Siamese twins and
> at the same time undertook to furnish
> the brothers lodging when they needed
> it in Lyon. Sometimes the brothers
> stayed with the Catins, sometimes with
> other safe houses in Lyon. Madame
> Catin did excellent work as a courier,
> was completely trustworthy and

indefatigable in the question of rail travel, which at that time was most difficult and tiring. She was arrested early in 1943 with the brothers and with a certain Madame Besen, at whose home they were staying at the time. Madame Catin was sent to Fresnes, then Compiègne, to Ravensbrück, and finally to concentration camp Holleischen in Czechoslovakia, between Pilsen and Prague. Monsieur Catin, warned that his wife had been arrested, took to the mountains for a certain time, and upon his return to Lyon, found that the Germans had been to their flat and emptied it of clothes, furniture, pots and pans, leaving the bare walls. Madame Catin was liberated by the American army at Holleischen and returned to Lyon in May 1945. In view of the excellent work done by Madame Catin and the fact that all her possessions have been taken away by the Germans, I would recommend in addition to a letter of appreciation for her work that she be given financial assistance in so far as is compatible with the policy of the office to help her reestablish a home. Madame Catin could be given thirty thousand francs for services she has rendered as a courier, and in lodging and caring for the brothers during difficult times.

There were many similar letters.

"I've found a jeep!" Paul told Virginia. "We can leave today if you want."

On June 17, 1945, Virginia and Paul set off on a 1,000 mile trip through France to discover the fate of former Resistance members who had served so faithfully. Another purpose of the trip was to collect radio equipment still in the districts. Virginia had kept careful records of the disposition of every piece of equipment that had come into her hands.

One of their first stops was the office of Dr. Rousset. "Greetings, dear friend," he hugged Virginia. Years in a concentration camp had taken their toll. He was gray-faced and rail thin, but the twinkle in his wise old eyes remained. On November 13, 1942, the doctor had been arrested, sent to a prison near Paris, and kept in solitary confinement for a year. He was then sent to the infamous Buchenwald concentration camp. There he worked as a doctor, continuing his Resistance work while duplicating and hiding medical files showing the inhuman treatment of American and British prisoners. He gave the files to the US Third Army Corps, who eventually liberated the camp.

Sheer rage was Virginia's reaction to the fate of the kind and generous Dr. Rousset, as he told of life in the camps. The good doctor's problem was he was too trusting. Unfortunately, he trusted Abbé Alesh.

Virginia's suspicions about the abbé turned out to be correct. Abbé Alesh had completely fooled Dr. Rousset, who did not doubt for a moment that he was who he said he was.

With the end of the war, it seemed the abbé had disappeared. He had gone to Brussels and used forged letters of recommendation to get a job as a chaplain at a refugee center. He worked at the center from November 1944 until he was arrested by Allied forces in May 1945. He confessed that through him the Germans were able to learn a great deal about Virginia Hall's network and activities, and that he knew Virginia suspected him of being a German spy. He was turned over to the French to be tried for his crimes.

Taking their leave of Dr. Rousset, Virginia and Paul visited district after district where she was greeted as an old friend. Fortunately, most of those who had helped were unharmed and in fair to good health. However, like Madame Catin, many had lost everything they owned and were living in abject poverty.

Madame Joulian and her husband were arrested and tortured for information about the Limping Lady and the Resistance. She was released after two months with her front teeth knocked out, a broken arm, and suffering from poor health. Monsieur Joulian was sent to Austria to work in a German defense industry. The Joulians lost their factory in Lyons and returned home to bare walls, as did Germaine Guérin who was also sent to a concentration camp. Her friend, Monsieur Genet, was beaten and tortured, and died in a cattle car taking 150 prisoners to a concentration camp.

Monsieur Labourier and his wife were both imprisoned, and his entire fleet of trucks was confiscated. He and his wife, once prosperous members of the community, were now clothed in rags, with no money to replace all they had lost.

Virginia Hall and Paul Goillot returned to Paris in late June 1945. Two months later, both returned to the United States where the two good friends parted ways.

There was a letter waiting in Baltimore for Virginia from Bill Donovan, head of the American OSS. Colonel James R. Forgan, OSS commanding officer in the European Theatre of Operations, had nominated Virginia for the Distinguished Service Cross, the US Army's highest military decoration after the Medal of Honor. No other civilian in World War II received such a nomination.

General Donovan, in telling President Truman the extraordinary work Virginia had performed, suggested the president might want to personally award the medal. President Truman agreed. The ceremony should be held at the White House with photographers present. Virginia's deeds and bravery should be known to the country at large.

"NO!" Virginia said. "First of all, it is ridiculous to receive a medal for doing the job one was expected to do. Second, I consider myself an active agent in the field and front-page publicity would render my work useless. Future intelligence work would be impossible."

General Donovan agreed. He presented the Distinguished Service Cross to Virginia in a private ceremony in his office on September 23, 1945. Mrs. Hall, Virginia's mother, was the only other person present.

The citation that accompanied the Medal read:

Miss Virginia Hall, an American
civilian in the employ of the Special
Operations Branch, Office of Strategic
Services, voluntarily entered and
served in enemy occupied France from

March to September, 1944. Despite
the fact that she was well known
to the Gestapo because of previous
activities, she established and maintained
radio communication with London
Headquarters, supplying valuable
operational and intelligence information,
and with the help of a Jedburgh team,
she organized, armed, and trained three
battalions of French Resistance forces
in the Department of the Haute-Loire.
Working in a region infested with enemy
troops and constantly hunted by the
Gestapo, with utter disregard for her
safety and continually at the risk of
capture, torture, and death, she directed
the Resistance forces with extraordinary
success in acts of sabotage and
guerrilla warfare against enemy troops,
installations, and communications.
Miss Hall displayed rare courage,
perseverance, and ingenuity; her efforts
contributed materially to the successful
operations of the Resistance forces in
support of the Allied Expeditionary
Forces in the liberation of France.

*Virginia Hall received the Distinguished Service Cross
from General William Donovan, chief of the
Office of Strategic Services, on September, 23, 1945.*
National Archives, Records of the Office of Strategic Services

While she politely thanked the general, Virginia did not feel she had done anything to deserve such an honor. She had simply done the job that was expected of her, as had so many others who should be recognized.

Her final report submitted to the OSS cited many French citizens who risked their lives to help her in her work:

- Farmer Lopinat, who provided refuge and protection in the Creuse and who was willing to help in any way.
- Madame Long and her son, Francois, who gave shelter and aid in Paris.
- Colonel and Madame Vessereau, who took me in at Cosno, and the colonel became my right-hand man there.
- Madame Estelle Bertrand at Sury-on-Lore, who took me into her house and gave advice as regards to the people of the countryside.
- Dede Zurbach, my man Friday, who had perhaps the hardest job of all working for a slave driver, and who acquitted himself most ably.
- Madame Boitier and son, Pierre. He was my electrical mechanic, and she would drop everything on a moment's notice to

travel with me when necessary, as would Madame Long.

- Madame Bruand and her daughter Therese placed their home at our disposal as a safe house.
- Commandant Thorond, who acted as treasurer and paymaster in the Haute-Loire, a very able, honest man who, unfortunately, resigned as soon as I left.
- Madame Leah Lebret at Le Chambon-sur-Lignon took care of me in the Haute-Loire, gave me a room, and let me work at the farm. She later fed me and many others. She deserves special mention.
- Monsieur André Girard of the Salvation Army at Le Chambon-sur-Lignon gave me an abandoned house to live in.
- Lieutenant Bob (La Boulicaud), who has done a swell job and stood by me like a brick through any amount of trouble.

The last item in the "Activity Report of Virginia Hall," American intelligence agent, was No. 15, which asked, "Were you decorated in the field?"

"No," she had typed. "No reason to be."

On October 1, 1945, the OSS was no more. President

Truman signed an order dissolving the organization, feeling the FBI was the only intelligence agency the country needed.

"Thank goodness," said Mrs. Hall. "Virginia will finally be returning home."

"Sorry," Virginia told her mother. "Retirement to Box Horn Farm is out of the question. Surely with my background and proven record, there will be a job for me now in the Foreign Service."

In March 1946, Virginia applied for a position in the US Department of State's Foreign Service.

"I served with the Foreign Service from 1931 to spring 1939," she wrote, "and am familiar with and have performed nearly all of the duties expected in the consular service."

Her application might have received more attention if she had included the citation written by her London boss, Maurice Buckmaster: "A remarkable woman of extraordinary courage and formidable tenacity. Despite her transatlantic accent, her memorable appearance, her wooden leg, she succeeded in remaining almost three years in occupied territory without being arrested. She did not submit easily to discipline and she had the habit of forming her ideas without regard to the views of others, but she rendered inestimable services to the Allied cause and is a very great friend of France."

Unbelievably, the response was once again NO! An appointment could not be considered, this time because of budgetary restrictions.

Virginia was furious. However, she was not surprised when it was soon evident that, while the FBI could handle homeland affairs, another agency was needed to deal with intelligence activities on foreign soil. The Central Intelligence Agency (CIA) was born.

Virginia applied and was immediately accepted as a field representative. In this new job, she had at last achieved her dream. She was representing the United States all over the world, from Albania to Yugoslavia, from South America to Asia. She prepared war plans for the Southern European Division, action plans for South Asia, headed the paramilitary desk for France, and took on numerous other roles, gathering intelligence to help keep the peace throughout the world. When she wasn't traveling, she had a desk at the CIA Headquarters in Washington, DC, that allowed her to spend an occasional weekend at her beloved Box Horn Farm.

It was on one of these weekends in 1947, just after returning from a European tour, that Virginia heard a car in the driveway and was surprised at the arrival of a smiling Paul Goillot. "Couldn't stay away," he laughed.

"I'm glad," she responded.

For the next three years, Virginia and Paul continued

to see each other between her overseas assignments. One assignment, with Radio Free Europe in 1948, put Virginia in New York City for a year. She and Paul were seen together frequently.

Friendship and respect turned to love and, in April 1950, Paul and Virginia were married in a quiet ceremony before a judge. She was forty-four years old, Paul was thirty-six. Virginia continued her work with the CIA for sixteen more years until mandatory retirement in 1966 at age sixty. Virginia and Paul spent their remaining years on a Maryland farm they purchased together, where Paul practiced his skill as a French chef, and Virginia raised flowers and cared for numerous pets. In her later years, the lady who loved danger existed quite peacefully on the farm with her beloved Paul until her death July 12, 1982, at age seventy-six.

The dream of the fourteen-year-old to serve her country in foreign lands, to meet foreign dignitaries, and to show the world that the United States stands ever willing to help those in need was indeed fulfilled, although not quite in the way Virginia had anticipated.

Most of those passing the simple headstone in the Druid Ridge Cemetery in Pikesville, Maryland, have no knowledge of the extraordinary woman who rests there.

ABOUT THE AUTHOR

Nancy Polette has written more than 150 books. She is a professor of education at Lindenwood University in St. Charles, Missouri. She taught elementary school for thirty years and directed gifted programs for St. Louis County Schools. *School Library Journal* describes her as "an educator with imagination, creativity, and an appreciation for the intelligence of children."

Nancy researched the life of Virginia Hall for five years to write this book.

She lives in O'Fallon, Missouri, a suburb of St. Louis. Learn more about her at www.nancypolette.com.

REFERENCES

Reports, Letters, Articles, Radio Addresses, and Unpublished Materials

Citation for Distinguished Service Cross, 27 September 1945. NARA Record Group 226, National Archives Building, Washington, DC.

CRI Form, Personal Information completed by Virginia Hall, 2 February 1943. British Archives, London, UK.

Dasey, Dennis. 1995. "Limping Lady Begins Spy Career in Early 1940s." Air Intelligence Agency, Kelly Air Force Base, San Antonio, TX.

De Gaulle Radio Address, 19 June 1940. http://www.spartacus.schoolnet.co.uk/FRresistance.htm

Death Notice, Virginia Hall Goillot, 13 July 1982. *Baltimore Sun*, Baltimore, MD.

Final Report of Virginia Hall, France Theatre of Operations. NARA Record Group 190, Box 347, Folder 240, National Archives Building, Washington, DC.

Hall Report, February 1942. Hall file, British Archives, London, UK.

Letter from Charlotte Norris to Mrs. Hall, 2 June 1944. CIA.

Letter from Cordell Hull, 25 January 1938. Hall File 123, NARA Record Group 59, National Archives Building, Washington, DC.

Letter to Maurice Buckmaster from Virginia Hall, 15 January 1941. Hall File, British Archives, London, UK.

Letter to Maurice Buckmaster from Virginia Hall; Request to Return to France, 1 October 1943. Hall File, British Archives, London, UK.

Letter to Virginia Hall from Maurice Buckmaster; Request to Return to France, 6 October 1943. Hall File, British Archives, London, UK.

Memo of Transfer of Virginia Hall from SOE to the OSS, 31 March 1944. British Archives, London, UK.

Order of the Day, 2 June 1944.
http://www.spartacus.schoolnet.co.uk/FRresistance.htm

Pétain Radio Address, 19 June 1940.
http://www.spartacus.schoolnet.co.uk/FRresistance.htm

Prologue, Winter 1944. 26:4.

Records of the Office of Strategic Services, NARA Record Group 226, National Archives Building, Washington, DC.

Report from Philomene (Virginia Hall) to British SOE on Capture of British Agents, 5 November 1942. British Archives, London, UK.

SOE Orders for Virginia Hall to Proceed to Spain as a Foreign Correspondent for the *Chicago Times*, 5 May 1943. British Archives, London, UK.

Virginia Hall Activity Report Describing Her New Identity and Location in France as a Milkmaid, 30 September 1944. NARA Record Group 190, Box 347, Folder 240. National Archives Building, Washington, DC.

Virginia Hall, OSS, Theatre Service Record, 27 January 1945. Hall File, British Archives, London, UK.

Books

Binney, Marcus. 2003. *The Women Who Lived for Danger.* New York: William Morrow.

Buckmaster, Maurice. 1958. *They Fought Alone*. London: Odhams Press.

Churchill, Peter. 1953. *Duel of Wits*. New York: Putnam.

Cookridge, E.H. 1966. *Inside the S.O.E.* London: Heinemann.

Dear, Ian. 1999. *Sabotage and Subversion: The SOE and OSS at War*. London: Cassell Military Paperbacks.

Foot, M.R.D. 1966. *SOE in France: An Account of the Work of the British Special Operations Executive in France 1940–1944*. London: HMSO.

Howarth, Patrick. 2000. *Undercover: the Men and Women of the S.O.E.* London: Phoenix Press.

Jackson, Julian. 2001. *France: The Dark Years, 1940–1944*. Oxford: Oxford University Press.

Lyle, Stuart. 1953. *Secret Life of Walter Winchell*. New York: Boar's Head Books.

Mahoney, M.H. 1993. *Women in Espionage: A Biographical Dictionary*. Santa Barbara, CA: ABC CLIO, Inc.

McIntosh, Elizabeth. 1998. *Sisterhood of Spies: The Women of the OSS*. New York: Dell Publishing, Random House.

Payment, Simone. 2004. *American Women Spies of World War II*. New York: The Rosen Publishing Group.

Rossiter, Margaret. 1991. *Women in the Resistance*. Santa Barbara, CA: Praeger, ABC CLIO, Inc.

Ruby, Marcel. 1988. *F Section: SOE: The Buckmaster Networks*. London: Leo Cooper Ltd.

West, Nigel. 1992. *The Secret War: the Story of the S.O.E.* London: Hodder and Stoughton.